D0250986

UNIVERSAL RIGHTS
DOWN TO EARTH

AMNESTY INTERNATIONAL GLOBAL ETHICS SERIES

General Editor: Kwame Anthony Appiah

In December 1948, the UN General Assembly adopted the United Nations Universal Declaration of Human Rights and thereby created the fundamental framework within which the human rights movement operates. That declaration—and the various human rights treaties, declarations, and conventions that have followed—are given life by those citizens of all nations who struggle to make reality match those noble ideals.

The work of defending our human rights is carried on not only by formal national and international courts and commissions but also by the vibrant transnational community of human rights organizations, among which Amnesty International has a leading place. Fifty years on, Amnesty has more than three million members, supporters, and subscribers in 150 countries, committed to campaigning for the betterment of peoples across the globe.

Effective advocacy requires us to use our minds as well as our hearts; and both our minds and our hearts require a global discussion. We need thoughtful, cosmopolitan conversation about the many challenges facing our species, from climate control to corporate social responsibility. It is that conversation that the Amnesty International Global Ethics Series aims to advance. Written by distinguished scholars and writers, these short books distill some of the most vexing issues of our time down to their clearest and most compelling essences. Our hope is that this series will broaden the set of issues taken up by the human rights community while offering readers fresh new ways of thinking and problem-solving, leading ultimately to creative new forms of advocacy.

FORTHCOMING AUTHORS:

Jonathan Wolff

John Broome

Philip Pettit

John Ruggie

Sheila Jasanoff

Martha Minow

ALSO BY RICHARD THOMPSON FORD

Rights Gone Wrong:
How Law Ignores Common Sense and Undermines Social Justice

The Race Card: How Bluffing About Bias Makes Race Relations Worse

Racial Culture: A Critique

3 3052 09804 1983

UNIVERSAL RIGHTS DOWN TO EARTH

Richard Thompson Ford

W. W. NORTON & COMPANY

NEW YORK LONDON

HARMONY LIBRARY
Fort Collins, Colorado

Copyright © 2011 by Richard Thompson Ford

All rights reserved
Printed in the United States of America
First Edition

For information about permission to reproduce selections from this book,
write to Permissions, W. W. Norton & Company, Inc.,
500 Fifth Avenue, New York, NY 10110

For information about special discounts for bulk purchases, please contact
W. W. Norton Special Sales at specialsales@wwnorton.com or 800-233-4830

Manufacturing by Courier Westford
Production manager: Anna Oler

Library of Congress Cataloging-in-Publication Data

Ford, Richard T. (Richard Thompson)
Universal rights down to earth / Richard Thompson Ford. — 1st ed.
p. cm. — (Amnesty international global ethics series)
Includes bibliographical references and index.
ISBN 978-0-393-07900-5 (hardcover)
1. Human rights—Social aspects. 2. Human rights—
Social aspects—Case studies. 3. Human rights—Political aspects.
4. Human rights—Political aspects—Case studies. I. Title.
JC571.F629 2011
323—dc23
                                  2011038042

W. W. Norton & Company, Inc.
500 Fifth Avenue, New York, N.Y. 10110
www.wwnorton.com

W. W. Norton & Company Ltd.
Castle House, 75/76 Wells Street, London W1T 3QT

1 2 3 4 5 6 7 8 9 0
HARMONY LIBRARY
Fort Collins, Colorado

*To Marlene: who proves that idealism
and pragmatism can peacefully coexist.*

CONTENTS

UNIVERSAL RIGHTS
DOWN TO EARTH

INTRODUCTION

The United Nations Convention on the Elimination of All Forms of Discrimination against Women (CEDAW) requires signatory nations to "incorporate the principle of equality of men and women in their legal system, abolish all discriminatory laws and . . . ensure elimination of all acts of discrimination against women by persons, organizations or enterprises." This is an ambitious agenda, encompassing law reform and the regulation of private parties. Nonetheless, a surprising number of nations—including many without robust civil rights traditions and with cultures of deep-seated and pervasive gender hierarchy, such as Afghanistan and Saudi Arabia—have ratified it.

To the chagrin of feminists and human rights advocates, the United States has not ratified CEDAW, a distinction it shares only with the Vatican, Iran, Somalia, Sudan, and a few small island nations. Among the nations that have ratified CEDAW are Yemen, Burma (Myanmar), North Korea, and Saudi Arabia. This should be somewhat embarrassing for the putative leader of the free world, but, as a practical matter, what does it mean? Is the day-to-day life of the typical woman in, say, Saudi Arabia better than that of a typical American woman? The United States has not come close to eliminating all forms of discrimination against women, but hasn't it done a better job than Afghanistan—where girls are routinely threatened with violence for daring to attend school—or Saudi Arabia? Saudi Arabia insists that women enjoy the same rights as men under its laws, but women—and only women—are required to wear veils and shoulder-to-toe covering when in public, are forbidden to drive automobiles, and are regularly refused service in restaurants unless accompanied by a man. Saudi law provides that sons receive double the inheritance of their sisters. By contrast, the United States has some of the world's most comprehensive and well-enforced laws against sex discrimination, and American women enjoy more personal freedom and opportunity than do women in much of Europe and most of the rest of the world. American civil rights laws are far from perfect, but the United States has eliminated most formal legal distinctions based on sex, and American businesses face the threat of costly litigation if they discriminate against women. Should it worry us that human rights commitments correspond so poorly to actual practices?

Despite this and many other conspicuous gaps between ideal and implementation, universal human rights represent the dominant utopianism of our era. Where previous generations put their hopes in spiritual enlightenment, political revolution, or technological emancipation, today's idealists look with anticipation to a world governed by human rights—a moral utopia of law. What would lead us to hope that the expression of a commitment to human rights would make a practical difference in the lives of human beings worldwide—regardless of the political and economic institutions they encounter? For much of human history, few thought so. Expressions of human rights, in one form or another, can be found at least as early as the great national revolutions in the eighteenth century, and some would argue that many of the earliest laws included human rights, albeit traveling under other names. But these earlier expressions of universal rights—the most dramatic of which was France's Declaration of the Rights of Man—did not imagine that human rights would change the behavior of governments as a practical matter, even if they insisted on rights that transcended states and sovereigns as a conceptual matter. The universal nature of rights was a reason for the overthrow of unjust governments—not an occasion for limiting their abuses. The rights of man were inextricably bound to the rights of the citizen and to the nature of government. Universal rights justified replacing oppressive regimes with new forms of government that would respect rights by design: monarchies and aristocracies, with republics and democracies. Even after the horrors of World War II, to which many attribute the birth of modern human rights, those concerned with social justice looked to political emancipation—not rights—to improve the human condition.

Today we are in the midst of something new: not only a belief that all humans have certain rights as a matter of theology or moral philosophy but also the belief that they have them as a matter of law and practical politics. Modern human rights are a unique fusion of universal morality, political activism, and legal formalism: an approach to social justice that codifies moral intuitions and seeks to enforce them through a combination of political lobbying, public relations campaigning, and litigation.

There's something reassuringly modest and pragmatic about human rights activism—it lacks the reckless utopianism of the counterculture and the quixotic ambition of revolutionary struggle. The human rights activist seeks not to overthrow or even reform governments; it seeks only to constrain them. Such activism does not need a political theory of the good or just state, only an account of the obligations of all states. But there's also something remarkably optimistic in human rights activism: a belief that moral ideals can be turned into enforceable rules and that globe-trotting hall monitors can save the world through a relentless and pervasive series of microinterventions—"one individual at a time," to borrow a slogan.

It can be hard to find a concise description of the practical goals and theoretical commitments of the human rights movement, in part because it is diffuse, nondogmatic, and antiprogrammatic. At times, formal law provides an account of its ambitions: hence, Amnesty International describes as its ambition "for every person to enjoy all of the rights enshrined in the Universal Declaration of Human Rights and other international human rights standards." But, I suspect, much of the charisma of human rights comes from the implicit presumption that its goals are self-evident and in no need of explication. Hence, most human rights organizations content themselves with a combination of general commitments, moral aphorisms, and specific examples of wrongs that need righting. But if one were to attempt to write a brief manifesto, it might read something like this:

> We may not be able to overthrow tyrannical regimes, and we may not have a comprehensive plan for good government worldwide. We know from bitter experience that revolutionary programs are too often an excuse for new tyrants to replace the old

ones. We don't seek to impose the best political system on other nations because we aren't sure there is one political system that would be best for all societies—there are many legitimate differences in culture and beliefs that justify different types of political regimes. But there are certain things that all human beings share and they imply a few fundamental limits that all tolerable governments must respect and a few fundamental values that all decent governments must advance. Over the years these fundamental limits and values have been codified as human rights. Most or all civilized nations have agreed on these rights, which is in and of itself evidence that they are of universal applicability. A decent government may be a republic or a monarchy, a parliamentary democracy or a one-party state; it may have a market economy based on free enterprise or state-controlled distribution of goods—these are all things on which reasonable people differ and the virtues of which may vary depending on circumstance. But no decent state may torture its citizens, or suppress political dissent, or persecute members of religious or ethnic minorities. All decent states must provide enough food for their people, or ensure that it is provided by private means; it is intolerable for government to oppress or victimize women or allow their victimization and oppression to occur without sanction. This is not an exhaustive list, but it is a representative one. Although we have renounced the naïve utopianism of past eras, we hold fast to a less ambitious but still vital humanism that condemns the worst and most unambiguous of abuses and affirms the most basic human needs.

Something much like this has gained more adherents than the demanding dogmas of many major religions, to say nothing of the rigorous doctrines of Marx, Fourier, Hayek, or Habermas. When Amnesty International first began its work on behalf of imprisoned political dissidents, human rights was a relatively limited and modest attempt to improve the lot of humankind, competing for attention and allegiance with antiracist struggle, postcolonial revolution, Pan-Africanism, environmentalism, antiwar activism, feminism, religious ministry, democratic socialism, anticommunism, and simple charity. Today it has outlived or subsumed many of these efforts. As a result, problems and crises that once were understood in terms of political conflict, oppression, exploitation, economic inefficiency, scarcity, or the limitations of technology are now often described in terms of human rights.

For example, the International Covenant on Economic, Social and Cultural Rights prescribes the "right of everyone to social security, including social insurance" and "to . . . fair wages ensuring a decent living for himself and his family . . . rest and leisure." This convention has taken on increasing urgency and importance along with human rights in general, replacing more comprehensive political solutions to social and economic injustice. The United States is, again, notable for its failure to ratify it. Amnesty International notes that "the Reagan and Bush administrations took the view that economic, social and cultural rights were not really rights but merely desirable social goals and therefore should not be the object of binding treaties." This recalls the opinion of the English parliamentarian Edmund Burke, who attacked the French Declaration of the Rights of Man by asking: "What is the use of discussing a man's abstract right to food or medicine? The question is upon the method of procuring and administering them. In that deliberation I shall always advise to call in the aid of the farmer and the physician rather than the professor of metaphysics."[1] Apropos of the International Covenant on Economic, Social and Cultural

Rights, perhaps Burke would recommend the services of labor economists, sociologists, and anthropologists.

International human rights are a distinctive type of law that must function primarily through informal and diplomatic means. While domestic civil rights can be imposed by force on the recalcitrant, there is no international sovereign to enforce international law—this has been one of the defining concerns of international legal theorists. But this doesn't mean that international law is impotent. It's simplistic to think that law only counts when it's backed by a cop with a gun. Law functions as much by changing social mores as by the threat of coercion. Indeed, any law that fails to inspire popular respect fails generally. Even though international human rights usually can't be imposed by force, they can be enforced through diplomatic pressure, economic sanctions, and bad press that threatens coveted national prestige. There may be no sovereign to enforce the letter of the law, but there is an army of bureaucrats, lawyers, diplomats, nongovernmental organizations, advisers, consultants, economists, pundits, and activists on hand to articulate principles, elucidate norms, enumerate protocols, debate implementation strategies, and document best practices. There's a multinational network of governmental expertise. This is how international law (and increasingly domestic law as well) works. The sovereign state is an important player, but it is only one of many players in the drama of global governance. Here I borrow an idea from the French social theorist Michel Foucault:

> with government it is a question not of imposing law on men but of disposing things: that is, of employing tactics rather than

laws, and even of using laws themselves as tactics—to arrange things in such a way that, through a certain number of means, such-and-such ends may be achieved.[2]

Law professor Janet Halley calls this a "governance" style of international law.[3] Here human rights organizations do not just speak truth to power, they exercise power along with a host of other organizations and institutions that control the movement of people and resources and the articulation of behavioral norms. Human rights groups don't impose laws on governments—instead, *pace* Foucault, they use laws as tactics in order to achieve ends that may or may not be apparent from the text of the legal instrument in question. For instance, Halley points out that laws against sexual trafficking are used to suppress not just abduction and forced sex but sex work generally. I will explore this question in some detail in part 2 of this book. Human rights in the mode of governance raise important—and at times troubling—questions, but they leave no doubt that international human rights can be quite effective despite the absence of the kind of direct, coercive enforcement that typically backs up domestic law.

Universal human rights offer an inspiring theme around which activists can organize and find common cause, and because the idea of rights combines moral conviction and legal entitlement, rights also offer the hope of relatively prompt practical efficacy often lacking in utopian social movements. This makes it tempting to describe any number of political and social ambitions in terms of universal rights. But as the list of "basic human rights" lengthens, the core idea of universal rights—compelling in its simplicity and modesty—faces an expanding set of pressures and contradictions. A small but growing number of legal scholars, historians, and political theorists have begun to look at human rights with a somewhat critical eye: the kind of gaze one expects to be directed at any ambitious political or social agenda. The common insight of these typically friendly critiques is that human rights are not natural, predetermined, or inevitable—they are the product of a specific and in many ways peculiar moment in history and the result of rhetorical and political decisions.

I am not a human rights lawyer or scholar of international human rights; most of my study has been in the area of American civil rights and race relations, jurisprudence, and American public law. In these areas there has been a great deal of discussion and debate on the question of rights. For instance, in the 1980s, legal scholars and political theorists associated with the leftist intellectual movement Critical Legal Studies advanced a comprehensive critique of rights. They argued that rights offered a false hope of social change through courts and litigation, that they siphoned energy from more promising political struggles, and that they distorted political and social consciousness by encouraging people to think of themselves as isolated rights-holders rather than as participants in collective endeavors. This inspired a spirited response from many people of color and feminists in defense of rights—civil rights in particular—which they insisted were indispensable to the moral growth of the nation and a defining part of the identity of minority groups. A series of more specific and less sweeping critiques of rights grew out of this debate: instead of making claims about rights generally, the next generation of critique offered detailed accounts of the costs and benefits of specific claims of right. One lesson of this interchange is that rights imply a distinctive type of analysis that is better suited to some questions than to others. This suggests that general and sweeping critiques of rights are probably mistaken, but that a rights-based approach may well be ineffective or counterproductive in some circumstances.

This short book will proceed in this vein, bringing some of the insights of the analysis of domestic civil rights law to the more varied and chaotic field of international human rights. It is dedicated to a relatively simple inquiry: What is gained (and what is lost) by describing a question as a matter of universal rights? As we enter what may well turn out to be the "human rights century," several questions about the scope, efficacy, and potential costs of human rights are becoming pressing.

1. Are Rights Universal?

International human rights are part of a tradition of optimistic humanism that seeks to transcend national, ethnic, and cultural chauvinism in favor of objective scientific and moral truths. They stand against the moral relativism of the disenchanted postmodernist and the provincial traditionalism of the social conservative. But is this ambition visionary or quixotic? Does the universalism of the human rights tradition follow from the undeniable interconnectedness of the modern global economy or is it struggling in vain against the resilience of religious division, national pride, and ethnic distinctiveness—still very much defining features of the modern world? Are international human rights more like the World Wide Web or Esperanto?

It is worthwhile to insist that all humans, whatever their place of origin or residence, ought to enjoy certain basic liberties and privileges. We should not sit still for the type of lazy relativism that would suggest that women in Saudi Arabia do not deserve the same freedoms that Western women enjoy, or that children in undeveloped nations are resigned to go to work rather than attend school. But, when carelessly expressed, universal rights tempt us to ignore the unique needs, limitations, and strengths of specific societies. Although human needs and human dignity do not vary from place to place, the conditions in which they can be achieved do. Rights must work with existing political institutions, social customs, and economic resources. In this sense, all human rights are local.

2. Can Abstract Rights Guide Concrete Reforms?

Assuming some broadly defined shared goals (an admittedly heroic assumption), do human rights provide an effective way to pursue them? How do ambitious principles translate into effective policies? Do rights inspire us to focus on human needs that would otherwise go unnoticed, or do they distract us from the practical conflicts and costs involved in economic and political reform? Do rights offer a way for the relatively powerless to influence events typically controlled by governments and multinational businesses, or are rights themselves a medium through which powerful interests exercise power—in other words, a form of politics by other means? And if rights *are* politics by other means, don't they need to be evaluated in the same way that we evaluate politics generally: with an eye to practical effectiveness, unintended consequences, and opportunistic misuse?

The abstraction and absolutism of rights language can lead us to ignore the complexities, ethical ambiguities, risks, and potential downsides of the interventions necessary to guarantee specific entitlements. Rights are typically expressed in uncompromising terms: When we say people have a right to humane conditions or equal treatment, we don't normally qualify the

assertion to make allowances for conflicting interests or extenu-
ating circumstances. The whole point of calling something a
"right" is that it takes priority over potentially conflicting interests and requires that adverse circumstances be overcome.
Sometimes this is justified, but most of the time, balancing of
interests is the appropriate way of making decisions. It's only
in very rare and special cases that we should declare a given
interest absolute and inviolable, regardless of the cost to others.
Most interests—even very important ones—have to be weighed
against other conflicting interests and other competitors for limited resources. When we use rights rhetoric indiscriminately, we
short-circuit this difficult but necessary type of political judgment and risk ignoring legitimate interests that may be under-
mined by the right in question.

3. How Do Rights Affect Political Consciousness?

Rights can encourage a narrow self-conception that excludes
or diminishes the emancipatory potential of unscripted human
interaction and political engagement. As historian Samuel
Moyn argues, human rights have become the repository for the
utopian energy and imagination once devoted to other, most
overtly political social movements, such as anti-colonialism and
Marxism.[4] But rights are a peculiar receptacle for utopianism
because their logical structure is typically an individualistic and
legalistic one. Yes, there are arguments for group rights, but
it is telling that the very idea of group rights *requires* an argument for the departure from the common understanding that
rights are held by individuals. Yes, there are theories of rights
independent of law, but without law rights amount to little more
than strongly worded moral or political claims. Their distinc-

tiveness—and their distinctive power—derives from the potential for legal enforcement or at least a legalistic idea of their applicability. The rights-bearing person seeks vindication from above: conceptually from timeless moral absolutes and practically from courts, tribunals, international committees, nongovernmental organizations, and an imagined international community. As Moyn argues, morality displaces politics in the human rights imagination. Moreover, isolated appeals involving discrete injuries displace movements for comprehensive social and political change. Not only is such an individualistic moral utopianism likely to be quite limited in addressing what are, in the end, political problems; it also encourages a narrow political subjectivity in which appeals to conceptual abstractions and to outside authorities displace collective solutions and civic cooperation.

4. Can Too Many Rights Make a Wrong?

Overuse of rights rhetoric threatens to dilute the meaning of rights in those rare cases where an unequivocal and inviolable guarantee is appropriate. If too many political claims, however valid, are described as rights, it's inevitable that many "rights" will be subject to precisely the same political pressure and conflict that surround any other controversial demand or costly claim on limited resources. As a result, rights will be subject to the same kinds of compromises, trade-offs, and cost-benefit analyses that are characteristic of everyday politics. Once it becomes common to think of rights in this way—as politics by other means—their uniqueness will be lost. Talk of rights will simply be an especially formal and emphatic (but not especially nuanced) way of making a contestable political claim: what philosopher Jeremy Bentham referred to as "bawling on paper."

You'll notice that these questions do not begin with philosophical or moral principles—in one way or another, they all focus on results. Practically speaking, rights are meaningful only when they actually make a difference in the way people behave. It makes little sense to insist on rights that few will respect and even less sense to push for rights that sound good in theory but are likely to misfire in practice. The study of law is as much a study of its limitations as of its power—learning the law means learning how a legal intervention is likely to reverberate through a complex social and political milieu.

Practically speaking, a right is a legal entitlement that an individual or entity can enforce against someone else. People don't always have to go to court to enforce their rights; when rights are well established and accepted, we typically respect each other's rights as a matter of course. For instance, it is rare today that anyone in the United States needs to sue a lunch counter or hotel for the right to be served regardless of his or her race. Most proprietors respect the right of citizens to be free of race discrimination, both because they know it is the law and because most people have come to believe that race discrimination is morally wrong. But when civil rights laws were first passed, we did need lawsuits to enforce them, and today the threat of effective enforcement hangs over social and economic relationships, keeping bigots in line. We all do business in the shadow of the law, so to speak. Civil rights made a difference in two ways: They changed social norms, so most people comply as a matter of personal conviction and habit, and they remain available as formally enforceable mandates to discipline the recalcitrant.

I won't insist that this is the only way to think about rights—philosophy and normative theory help us to step back from the minutiae of administrative detail and focus our attention on questions of moral principle. But I will insist that a practical, results-oriented approach is a necessary complement to the theoretical abstractions that often define discussions of human rights.

In answering these questions, part 1 of the book will look at legal and philosophical discussions of human rights. At least since the American and French Revolutions, human rights have been a source of inspiration and hope for millions of people suffering under unjust, corrupt, or negligent political regimes. But for just as long there have been intelligent skeptics, who questioned the wisdom and practicality of human rights guarantees. Edmund Burke attacked the Declaration of the Rights of Man as abstract scholasticism divorced from the real needs of human beings and the lived history of national cultures. Burke's most enduring insight was that human societies are much too complicated to allow one to begin with an abstract principle or concept and try to reason one's way toward a correct legal result or sound public policy. Instead, one had to begin with what had worked well in the past and make incremental improvements. Although Burke is now known as the father of modern ideological conservatism, these insights should be congenial to any student of law and politics, regardless of ideological orientation. Jeremy Bentham dismissed the Rights of Man as "nonsense on stilts," writing forcefully against the notion of "imprescriptable" human rights and advancing a pragmatic conception of legal entitlements based on social utility. Bentham's insistence that rights must be evaluated by their practical social consequences in a specific context is a valuable insight, even if one questions or rejects Benthamite utilitarianism as a general ethical worldview.

The American legal realist Wesley Hohfeld insisted that "rights talk" too often betrayed analytic confusion about the precise nature of the entitlement asserted and the identity of the party that bore the obligation to guarantee it. And Karl Marx worried that human rights were a bourgeois mystification that, like capital, alienated human beings from themselves and from their fellow citizens and forestalled substantive political and economic change. Thomas Paine was a forceful advocate of human rights and provided a sharp response to Burke's skepticism, but his conception of rights was inseparable from comprehensive political change—indeed, it was primarily a justification for revolution and the overthrow of monarchies. What can these perspectives on rights from across the ideological spectrum tell us about the challenges and risks of international human rights today?

I suspect that readers preoccupied with ideology will find this approach disorienting: a citation of Burke marks one as a conservative writer; a reference to Marx indicates a leftist radical. What could it mean to cite both favorably? This is deliberate: I want to throw off-balance the reader who weighs all ideas on an ideological scale. I would argue that an ideological metric is especially misplaced in a discussion of human rights. After all, the defining genius of human rights is that they stand outside ideological partisanship. When Amnesty International began petitioning repressive governments to release prisoners of conscience, it was quite careful to avoid condemning the political organization or philosophy of the states in question; it well understood that no regime would accept a petition that challenged its defining commitments. Over the years, as human rights work has taken on more ambitious and complex causes, it has naturally drifted toward an ideological alliance with leftist and progressive causes. Those who support these causes may find this shift appealing, but there are perils in such an association: If human rights become associated with a specific ideology, they will lose their claim to moral priority and universal application. If human rights become a vehicle for liberal and progressive causes, why should conservatives respect them any more than they respect the liberal agenda driving them?

The uncharitable will insist that this use of diverse thinkers betrays a lawyer's promiscuity—a willingness to cite any authority that will further the argument. Perhaps, but it also reflects a valid insight that will animate my remarks in this book. What links these thinkers is their skepticism about abstract idealism and their insistence on the importance of social context, material conditions, and concrete results. This sociological orientation is indispensable to sound policy making and successful social advocacy—and much of modern human rights work is, in effect, policy making and social advocacy.

Accordingly, part 2 will examine violations of human rights and the application of human rights guarantees in several specific contexts. Migrant farm workers in southern Italy face exploitation, racism, xenophobia, and violence. These conditions are stark human rights violations, but arguably they are just symptoms of a centuries-old dysfunctional civic culture in which organized crime functions as a surrogate government. Do human rights make sense without a civil society in which rights and civic duties are habitual? India produces more than enough food to feed her people, but tons of grain rot in state-managed warehouses while millions starve. Will a right to food help India's desperate and destitute, or will it encourage the government to compound the harm its misbegotten policies have already caused? An aggressive human rights approach to human trafficking promises to thwart a horrific trade in human flesh by pressuring national governments to stop suspicious migration at the border. But these policies may actually have made it harder for some women to escape sexually exploitative situations overseas, by making them more vulnerable to exploitation by unscrupulous handlers who demand a share of future earnings and large fees to help them navigate increasingly onerous immigration processes. The Convention on the Elimination of All Forms of Discrimination against Women is an astounding human rights success if measured by the number of nations that have accepted it, but many nations seem to honor their commitment in the breach. In fact, some have used CEDAW to defend blatantly discriminatory laws and customs, turning their human rights commitments into a public relations opportunity. Do humanitarian goals find strength in numbers, even when many are only nominal supporters, or do strongly worded guarantees, often ignored, weaken all human rights by suggesting that compliance is a matter of interpretation and of convenience? Part 2 will end with a short summary of the findings and arguments of the book and will offer brief suggestions for a down-to-earth conception of universal human rights.

PART ONE

Rights in Theory

For almost as long as there have been rights, there have been misgivings, cavils, critiques, and outright attacks on the idea of rights. Many of these objections have been predictably self-serving and opportunistic: the complaints of arrogant sovereigns faced with new limits to their previously untrammeled authority or narrow-minded bureaucrats pressured to alter their plans to accommodate the needs of individual citizens. But there are also many thoughtful and principled critiques of rights, advanced by thinkers with varied political commitments. The most insightful critics do not critique rights in general; instead, they critique specific iterations of rights, while taking care to exempt and even defend others. For instance, Edmund Burke, the father of modern conservativism, heaped unsparing scorn on the notion of universal human rights, which he considered to be a pernicious scholastic abstraction, but he defended rights that grew out of a specific cultural and historical tradition, such as the "Rights of Englishmen" inscribed in the Magna Carta and reasserted during the Glorious Revolution. Jeremy Bentham, the author of modern utilitarianism, notoriously described the Declaration of the Rights of Man as "nonsense" and the idea of "imprescriptable" human rights as "nonsense upon stilts," but he took for granted that a just society and well-functioning legal order would respect many rights, which would vary according to circumstances. Karl Marx attacked "bourgeois rights" as a reification of human relationships that alienated citizens from each other and ultimately from their own deepest commitments and experiences. But his most famous discussion and critique of rights—"On the Jewish Question"—argues that respect for rights marks a profound advance in social and political development and begins with a compelling *defense* of rights to religious freedom.

Legal scholars have advanced detailed technical critiques of rights analysis, but again, the best of them have been specific and limited. American legal scholar Wesley Hohfeld argued that talk of rights was typically sloppy and imprecise: people evoke "rights" without specifying the precise legal entitlement at stake or the person or entity burdened by the corresponding obligation. His concern is just as valid today as it was when he was writing in the early twentieth century. For instance, many Americans believe that the First Amendment right to freedom of expression entitles an employee to keep her job after berating her employer or customers, but this confuses the nature of the entitlement with the identity of the guarantor. Americans enjoy the right to free speech, but the right obligates government, not private parties: an employer or property owner can restrict speech without offending the constitutional guarantee. Again, Hohfeld's insight does not suggest that rights are inherently misguided or imprecise—instead, it is simply a call to define and express claims of right with care.

In the 1980s, leftist scholars associated with the Critical Legal Studies movement argued that contemporary rights talk sapped the energy of social movements. Rights-based social activism effectively handed the direction of political change over to judges and other legal experts, who inevitably watered down the ambitions of the organic social movement. Rights also gave activists false hope, because what looked like an ironclad guarantee was in fact a malleable legal concept that could and would be reshaped according to practical expediency and the political predilections of the judges and bureaucrats charged with enforcement. Worst of all, they argued, rights offered a rigid and alienated conception of human social interaction, in which social relations are governed by formal roles and entitlements. For instance, rather than interacting as two people engaged in a common endeavor, rights require us to interact, first and foremost, as employer and employee; student and teacher; landlord and tenant. This critique suggested that rights were accompanied by a distinctive and limiting ideology that was incompatible with meaningful social change. But again, with rare exceptions, the legal critique of rights didn't propose eliminating legal entitlements; it called for a reevaluation of rights as a tool of political activism. The critique challenged the privileged centrality of rights in left-liberal political thought, not the idea of rights generally.

I'll look to these and other discussions to begin to address the four major questions about universal rights I posed in the introduction.

ARE RIGHTS UNIVERSAL?

One of the most enduring and central conceits of human rights thinking is that certain rights are universal in nature—they apply to everyone, everywhere. The earliest iterations of the idea of universal rights come from the natural law tradition: for believers in natural law, some legal rules and relations either are ordained by God or are inherent in human nature. The natural law tradition was once extremely influential—indeed, in the eighteenth century it was the dominant jurisprudence among European elites. Royalists and republicans debated whether natural law inscribed the divine right of kings or the inalienable rights of the citizen to self-determination. But natural law hasn't fared well in recent years—today most serious legal thinkers seek guidance in the positive law of legislation, civil code, common law, and written constitutions. Human rights are a notable exception: a good deal of the prestige of human rights derives from a vague but powerful idea that they reflect timeless absolutes, which stand above and apart from the specific treaties and conventions that give them concrete elaboration.

I won't engage the interminable debate among political philosophers and scholars of jurisprudence over whether certain human rights "exist" either as a matter of human nature or as a necessary precondition of a just and well-ordered society. And I leave to multiculturalists and their many and able detractors the vexing arguments over whether certain human rights are truly universal or whether the human rights tradition itself is a product of Western culture. In this book, I will focus on a different problem facing universal rights—the lack of an international civic culture to define rights and give them life. Here I must again evoke Edmund Burke and his reaction to the Declaration of the Rights of Man. Burke attacked the idea of the rights of *man* but offered a vigorous defense of the rights of *Englishmen*. There is a great deal in his discussion of those rights that we might reject, but Burke is convincing on two key points. The first: that robust and workable rights arise from the concrete circumstances of life and the specific lessons learned from struggle and conflict in a discrete social context. The second: that the development and application of such rights is best guided by common sense and good judgment—not by abstract reasoning.

Domestic civil rights often look like the application of abstract principle to diverse facts, but they almost always develop in reaction to some specific event or set of events in the life of a nation and then derive their legitimacy from that event. This is obvious whenever civil rights are under attack because their defenders quickly evoke the specific events that inspired them to beat back the assault ("that's just the sort of thing Lester Maddox said in defense of Jim Crow segregation!"). As a consequence, even though domestic civil rights may be set forth in abstract and general terms (such as *equal protection*), we have a pretty good idea what they mean because of the context in which they were developed. For instance, in the early 1970s Yale Law School professor Owen Fiss could insist with some confidence that the equal protection clause of the Fourteenth Amendment to the United States Constitution made blacks the "special wards" of the state and subjected laws that disadvantaged them to heightened judicial scrutiny because the history of slavery prompted the ratification of the Fourteenth Amendment and the history of Jim Crow racism and other race-based indignities and exploitation inspired its development and elaboration.[1] In context, the meaning of *equal protection* is clear enough. Of course there is still plenty of debate, but at least we have somewhere to begin and some warrant for insisting that separate public schools for black and white children constitutes a clearer violation than, say, separate restrooms for men and women.

The Civil Rights Act was modestly successful because the United States had in place a set of administrative agencies and a well-functioning and reasonably independent judicial system. American courts were used to applying vague civil rights guarantees to concrete disputes, having taken on the controversial job of constitutional review of legislation much earlier. By 1964, the American administrative state had reached maturity, with a growing number of federal, state, and local bureaucracies charged with implementing a host of complex regulatory schemes. Even with all of these advantages, civil rights implementation was spotty and fraught. For instance, school desegregation—perhaps the defining ambition of the African American civil rights struggle—was widely resisted and often unsuccessful. In 2006, two of every five black and Latino public school students attended a school that was more than 90 percent nonwhite,[2] and most American public schools are becoming more segregated with each passing year. I mention all of this not because the United States should serve as a model for human rights but only to provide one example of the cultural and institutional support that must underlie viable legal rights. Getting a government to articulate or endorse a human right is only a small part of the job: after that, the right must be defined in practical terms and implemented. This suggests that rights can never be universal as a practical matter; local institutions, laws, and customs are necessary for their implementation.

As early as the eighteenth century, when natural-law think-ing was at its zenith, the idea of universal and natural rights had its detractors. Edmund Burke thought natural rights existed but had little to do with government, while Jeremy Bentham insisted that there could be no rights without law and government. Both arrived at the same practical conclusion: Meaningful civil and human rights are legal entitlements guaranteed and enforced by government and as such they necessarily vary from society to society—practically speaking, there are no universal rights that transcend governments.

Bentham insisted that without government there is no law and without law, no rights: "We know what it is for men to live without government . . . no habit of obedience, and thence no government—no government, and thence no laws—no laws, and thence no such things as rights—no security—no property:— liberty, as against regular controul, the controul of laws and government—perfect; but as against all irregular controul, the mandates of stronger individuals, none. . . . security not more than belongs to beasts."[3] Bentham concluded that if we reject the savagery of the law of nature, then we must commit ourselves to a utilitarian approach in which law—including rights—is a matter of public convenience and must vary with particular circumstances in order to serve the common good.

Burke's conclusions are very similar to those of Bentham. For Burke, natural rights are the rights of people in the state of nature and hence have nothing to do with the practice of good government. Other than legal rights established by or accepted by governments, there is only the right of self-help as established by the law of the jungle. Government is not obligated to guarantee natural rights—in fact, it is organized in large part to provide security and prosperity by *restricting* natural rights:

> Government is not made in virtue of natural rights, which may and do exist in total independence of it, and exist in much greater clearness and in a much greater degree of abstract perfection; but their abstract perfection is their practical defect. By having a right to everything they want everything. . . . Society requires not only that the passions of individuals should be subjected, but that even in the mass and body, as well as in the individuals, the inclinations of men should frequently be thwarted, their will controlled, and their passions brought into subjection. . . . The moment you abate anything from the full rights of men, each to govern himself [without regard for others, in the brutal state of nature], and suffer any artificial, positive limitation upon those rights, from that moment the whole organization of government becomes a consideration of convenience. . . .[4]

By this Burke means that once we admit that we must limit the "natural" right to do whatever one pleases and accept the necessity of limits imposed by government, then natural rights are no longer relevant—the only question is how best to promote the happiness and welfare of everyone in society. This may well entail individual rights, but the establishment of those rights will of necessity vary, depending on national customs, habits, and circumstances.

Burke's insistence that rights must be specific to a given society follows from his belief that government is a consideration "of convenience" that allows for infinite variation. Since there is no one correct or obvious way of organizing government, he maintains, and since human affairs are unfathomably complex, it is impossible to reason one's way to the best—or even a tolerable—governmental structure. Good government is not designed—it evolves:

> The science of constructing a commonwealth, or renovating it, or reforming it, is, like every other experimental science, not to be taught a priori. . . . the real effects of moral causes are not always immediate; but that which in the first instance is prejudicial may be excellent in its remoter operation; and its excellence may arise even from the ill effects it produces in the beginning. The reverse also happens: and very plausible schemes, with very pleasing commencements, have often shameful and lamentable conclusions. In states there are often some obscure and almost latent causes, things which appear at first view of little moment, on which a very great part of its prosperity or adversity may most essentially depend. The science of government being therefore so practical in itself, and intended for such practical purposes—a matter which requires experience, and even more experience than any person can gain in his whole life, however sagacious and observing he may be—it is with infinite caution that any man ought to venture upon pulling down an

edifice which has answered in any tolerable degree for ages the common purposes of society. . . .[5]

So both Bentham and Burke reject any notion of universal human rights, as a practical matter. There are no natural human rights except, in Burke's belief, the right of unrestricted individual self-governance, which any sensible person would happily give up in exchange for the benefits of society. Rights can arise only from within a social context, and are justified— for Burke, by tradition, which reflects the collected wisdom of the ages—and for Bentham, by their utility in a specific social context. It would be foolish in the extreme to suspend or reform laws and customs justified by long-standing tradition or evident social utility based on the metaphysics of supposedly universal rights. Even if a given right has proven invaluable in one social context, it may be disastrous in another. For Burke, no amount of a priori philosophical justification can equal the combined wisdom of generations, which produced laws and habits well suited to the society in which they developed. For Bentham, no moral principle is universally and eternally valid—all principles must continually prove their social utility and any should unceremoniously be cast aside as soon as it no longer serves the common good.

Here there is an important difference between the thought of Burke and that of Bentham. Burke doesn't trust human judgment to evaluate and reform political institutions—he believes that human societies have too many moving parts for any reformer to predict accurately the consequences of reform. This of course counsels against revolution—which, with a few notable exceptions, Burke was certain threatened ruin—but it also suggests extreme caution about even modest reform. We can hear the echoes of Burke's cautiousness in today's antiregulation conservatives, who insist that liberal social-welfare programs and regulations often "hurt the people they are designed to help" due to unintended and unforeseen consequences. This can become an argument against any reform: tellingly, Burke counsels "infinite caution" when the object of reform has served society "in any tolerable degree."

By contrast, Bentham is more confident about the capacity of human beings to evaluate the likely effects of their political institutions—so much so, in fact, that he insists that "there is no right which, when the abolition of it is advantageous to society, should not be abolished." Indeed, one of Bentham's strongest objections to the notion of human rights is that they would restrict the freedom of future generations to reform the law. Hence Bentham mocks the proponents of universal rights, writing on their behalf:

> In us is the perfection of virtue and wisdom: in all mankind besides, the extremity of wickedness and folly. Our will shall consequently reign without controul, and for ever: reign now while we are living—reign after we are dead. All nations—all future ages—shall be . . . our slaves. Future governments will not have honesty enough to be trusted to the determination of what rights shall be maintained, what abrogated—what laws kept in force, what repealed. . . . Governments, citizens—all to the end of time—all must be kept in chains.[6]

Both Burke and Bentham believed that universal rights ignored the distinctiveness and diversity of human societies: for Burke, the distinctiveness of inherited social customs; for Bentham, a host of distinctive and ever-changing social conditions that demanded differing responses. But their sharply differing—indeed, almost diametrically opposed—ideas about the risks of human rights are instructive: for Burke rights threaten reckless and dangerous upheaval while for Bentham they threaten a tyranny of stasis, the dead hand of the past clenched into an iron fist.

Burke was right to worry that supposedly universal rights, thoughtlessly imposed, can upset the virtuous civic traditions and institutions of a nation. Moreover, rights—whatever their origin or justification—cannot succeed unless they find support in civil society and harmonize with existing customs, laws, and institutions. This does not mean that rights cannot also influence customs and promote reform of laws and institutions, but to do so they must build on other indigenous beliefs and norms. For example, rights—both international human rights and new interpretations of American civil rights—changed American racial customs, laws, and institutions in the 1950s and 1960s. World opinion, expressed in part through human rights, helped the American civil rights movement by providing a compelling language with which to condemn American racism. Americans—especially the American federal government, which was engaged in a fierce diplomatic struggle against communism—cared about world opinion, and Jim Crow racism was a source of embarrassment and shame. Communists pointed to American race relations as evidence of the moral corruption and hypocrisy of the West; in seeking alliances with Third World nations, the Soviet Union was quick to say, in essence: *Look at how the Americans treat their blacks—that is how they will treat you.* American civil rights succeeded by building on existing American commitments to civic equality and a growing belief in racial equality that emerged after World War II—which many Americans believed was fought in order to resist Nazi racism. The American civil rights movement could not have succeeded without drawing on these indigenous values and commitments.

Bentham's concern about stasis is also valid. Rights that may seem timeless often reflect the partial and limited vision of a specific historical moment. For instance, in the late nineteenth and early twentieth centuries, American courts held that labor organizing and picketing violated the property and contract rights of corporations and business owners. As legal historian Morton Horwitz observes: "In late-nineteenth-century orthodox legal thought, it was . . . possible to make statements such as 'a labor boycott is inconsistent with the right to property' or 'coercive picketing violates the employer's property rights and therefore should be enjoined.' "[7] Because these rights were thought to be universal and timeless—rooted in natural as well as in constitutional law—it took a legal revolution in thought (a "crisis," in Horwitz's terms) to undo these ideas and allow for the flourishing of the modern labor movement. The idea of absolute and inviolable property rights led the US Supreme Court to invalidate much of the New Deal, provoking President Franklin Delano Roosevelt to concoct the notorious "court-packing" scheme by which he planned to expand the size of the Supreme Court in order to overwhelm the recalcitrant justices with new members sympathetic to his progressive legislation. Faced with this crisis of legitimacy (and influenced by some new appointments made due to retirements), the court softened its position and the New Deal survived.

The history of American property rights vindicates Bentham's concern about rights-as-stasis. Very strong property and contract rights made sense as a reaction to the abuses of the British Crown, which included, infamously, seizing private land without compensation and unilaterally abrogating contracts on which parties had relied when making investments. But the absolute inviolability of property and contract rights was poorly suited to the rapidly industrializing nation that America had become in the early twentieth century. It was more and more apparent that government regulation of private affairs was necessary to facilitate national markets and build modern infrastructure, such as railroads. Courts carved out exceptions to the absolutist conception of property to allow railroads to use private land and destroy private property without compensating the owner, but they evoked an unequivocal property right to punish hapless trespassers and enjoin labor organizing. Increasingly, the absolutist conception of property and contract seemed to be reserved for large, moneyed interests. The New Deal was a sensible reaction to economic crisis and the interconnected nature of the modern economy—since government intervention was necessary to make a national market work for large businesses, it was only fair that government intervention should also protect average working people. Rights threatened to prevent government from responding to changing circumstances and to thwart social justice and economic progress. As Bentham feared, the notion of timeless rights had come to mean that "Future governments will not have honesty enough to be trusted to the determination of what rights shall be maintained, what abrogated—what laws kept in force, what repealed. . . ."

Some rights that seem beneficial in the abstract will be detrimental in practice, and some rights that are beneficial in one context will be destructive in another. To some extent, then, each nation—as well as each generation—must develop its own human rights, refracted through its unique institutions and reflecting its own traditions and circumstances. Perhaps Edmund Burke went too far when he argued that the rights were developed and passed on exclusively within a national community, "without any reference whatever to any other more general or prior right." But he was right to insist that rights must build on existing institutions and traditions and must develop in harmony with a healthy political system and sound public policy. And he was especially insightful in noticing that the appropriate "liberties and restrictions vary with times and circumstances and admit to infinite modifications, they cannot be settled upon any abstract rule; and nothing is so foolish as to discuss them upon that principle. . . ."

Universal rights can express general commitments, but they acquire practical significance only in specific local contexts. Just as a ray of light acquires visible color only when it strikes an object, the effect of human rights will depend on how they are reflected in the objective conditions of a specific local culture. Rights cannot make local cultures and institutions bend to fit them: indeed, the history of revolution amply demonstrates that even after a government is toppled and replaced, the *ancien régime* dies hard. Typically, the new order bears a family resemblance to the old, because culture is not as easily overthrown as a monarch and the habits of civil society are not as readily rewritten as a constitution. Human rights activism and diplomatic pressure will not accomplish what revolution and regime change cannot; for the most part, local civic culture must be taken as given. It follows that, as a practical matter, rights should and must vary with local cultures and institutions.

CAN ABSTRACT RIGHTS GUIDE CONCRETE REFORMS?

Aggressive human rights conventions express lofty ambitions that look good on paper, but they can fall far short in terms of substantive change on the ground. Nation-states face financial constraints that limit their ability to implement substantive positive rights, such as rights to housing, food, and economic security. Rights against discrimination that apply to private actors require government to spend scarce resources on enforcement. And human rights guarantees require the cooperation of the judicial and political branches of government over long periods of time to enact and enforce national legislation. Meaningful civil rights guarantees depend on the details of administration and enforcement and require changes in widespread cultural attitudes. But human rights conventions do not specify such administrative details or the policy changes required to bring about such cultural changes. Like a drunk who promises to quit cold turkey after a family intervention, the nation that subscribes to sweeping human rights guarantees under international pressure may have neither the resources nor, ultimately, the inclination to follow through in the long run. If many signatory nations—especially those without a strong domestic civil rights tradition—don't take their obligations seriously as a practical matter, perhaps the American refusal to ratify some human rights conventions reflects not a contemptible truculence but rather an admirable seriousness about rights: the United States refuses to ratify agreements that it cannot or will not faithfully execute.

It's a commonplace idea in modern jurisprudence that a legal right necessarily implies a remedy. Legal scholar Wesley Hohfeld criticized sloppy and casual uses of the term *right* in the 1920s, insisting that any useful assertion of a right required one to identify the precise legal interest at stake and the person or entity charged with the corresponding obligation to guarantee that interest. A clear implication is that it's not enough to say that one has (or should have) a right to something—one must also make the case that some specific person or entity can and should provide it.

Sometimes the case is easy to make. If political dissidents

have a right to criticize their governments, the governments have the corresponding obligation to tolerate criticism. But sometimes the case is not so clear, and human rights rhetoric often proceeds by asserting the existence of rights first, and then identifying "violators" almost as an afterthought. For instance, the right to food, found in several different human rights conventions and treaties, seems to obligate nation-states. Indeed, most human rights obligate states, although recently there has been some movement to bring to account private parties, businesses, and other nonstate actors for human rights violations. But suppose states are incapable of providing adequate food for their citizens—or, worse yet, suppose state interventions actually make matters worse. Can other parties be sanctioned as well? Olivier De Schutter, the UN Special Rapporteur on the Right to Food, suggests that "financial speculation . . . on derivatives of essential food commodities" is to blame for volatile food prices. He adds: "The major economies should ensure that such derivatives are restricted as far as possible to qualified and knowledgeable investors who trade on the basis of expectations regarding market fundamentals, rather than mainly or only for short-term speculative gain."[8]

This is a perfectly sensible suggestion, but it's hard to jibe with a conventional idea of human rights. Notice that the focus remains ambivalently on states ("the major economies" are to restrict derivative speculation), in keeping with the conventional notion that human rights obligate states. But the real problem is one of complex and internationally interconnected financial markets, which, as the recent global economic crisis proves, are beyond the comprehension—and even more so the control—of state regulators. Perhaps it's the speculators themselves who have violated the right to food rather than the states that have failed to control them, but it seems a bit of a stretch to insist that the mathematics savant who, sitting in an office in Manhattan, designed a complex derivative that included agricultural securities has violated the rights of a poor person in India. And, of course, one person's "speculator" is another's "engine of capitalist investment"; the idea that complex financial instruments are an evil to be repressed was not widely accepted before the global recession of 2007 and remains controversial today. None of this suggests that speculators should be exempt from criticism or pressure, but the language of human rights adds little if anything to what are at bottom thorny questions of economics, market regulation, and socially responsible investing.

At times, human rights can seem like a wish list of desirable humanitarian goals, unencumbered in their lofty ambition by such grubby considerations as cost, political will, and institutional capabilities. Worse yet, the goals themselves often are unambiguously desirable only because they are described in such abstract terms that they can mean different things to different people. In this way, both practical objections and ideological conflict are banished, but precision and efficacy often slip over the border as well. For instance, the International Covenant on Economic, Social and Cultural Rights prescribes the "right of everyone to social security, including social insurance," and "to . . . fair wages ensuring a decent living for himself and his family . . . rest and leisure." Who could be against "fair wages," "a decent living," and "rest and leisure"? Will anyone make a case for unfair wages, an indecent living, and uninterrupted toil? But when the time comes to define terms and set priorities, all of the familiar problems of political economy must be addressed. How can the state or the international community ensure that wages are fair and living is decent? Is the solution state-imposed redistribution of resources, regulation of markets, or laissez-faire?

As Hohfeld pointed out, rights work best when they define

a discrete formal entitlement and identify a specific entity that can guarantee that entitlement. Rights to freedom of expression and political dissent, or against state-sponsored abuses, fit that description, and they are as important as ever in today's world of violent, tyrannical, and corrupt states. But other human rights often don't define a specific entitlement—instead, they blur important distinctions, such as that between an entitlement to be free of hindrance and an entitlement to affirmative aid in securing tangible goods—and they don't make it clear what entity bears the corresponding duty to guarantee the entitlement in question. Hohfeld attacked this kind of imprecision in the work of John Chipman Gray, who described rights using this example: "The eating of shrimp salad is an interest of mine, and, if I can pay for it, the law will protect that interest, and it is therefore a right of mine, to eat shrimp salad which I have paid for, although I know that shrimp salad always gives me the colic."[9]

Hohfeld pointed out that Gray confused two distinct legal interests—one in the "privilege" or liberty to eat the salad free of state interference or legal consequence (as opposed to the lack of such for someone who had stolen the salad) and the other in the right to eat the salad without interference from third parties:

A, B, C and D, being the owners of the salad, might say to X: "Eat the salad if you can; you have our license to do so, but we don't agree not to interfere with you." In such a case the privileges exist, so that if X succeeds in eating the salad, he has violated no rights of any of the parties. But . . . if A had succeeded in holding so fast to the dish that X couldn't eat the contents, no right of X would have been violated.[10]

This isn't inconsequential: A right that sounds attractive when vaguely formulated may in fact be unworkable in its specifics.

Moving from Hohfeld's shrimp salad to food more generally, a right to food seems morally compelling if we don't define it precisely and we focus only on the bearer of the right—the hungry person we imagine the right will feed. But once we think about the precise nature of such an entitlement and who should bear the duty to guarantee it, it begins to look more questionable. The conventional view is that human rights are guaranteed by the state; it follows, then, that states are responsible for guaranteeing a right to food. This is well and good if the right in question is one to be free of hindrance: the state must not prevent its citizens from feeding themselves by, say, legally penalizing the cultivation of crops or livestock. However, even this can get tricky: The law of private property effectively prevents the cultivation of land by anyone other than the owner and those to whom he or she gives permission; this effectively prohibits the cultivation of crops by most of the population, as the legal scholar Robert Hale pointed out in 1923.[11] It also makes sense to insist that states have a duty to make sure third parties don't keep people from food. Imagine an ethnic group that attempts to starve a rival group. But, of course, those entitlements are not enough. When many people in a country can't afford to purchase the food that is available on the open market, humanitarians insist, with good reason, that a right to food means what it seems to mean colloquially: People have a right to *get* food, not just an empty formal entitlement to eat the salad if they can get it. But at this point the duty in question is much more onerous and complex. Here, *pace* Burke, "the question is upon the method of procuring and administering. . . ." Most states are not well positioned to discharge this duty—indeed, as we shall see in examining the Indian case in part 2, the difficulties of popular politics and the inefficiencies of governmental bureaucracy may make the state an especially poor guarantor of many substantive goods.

Does this mean that humanitarians should have nothing to say about malnutrition and starvation? Of course not. But it does suggest that what we have to say may not be well put in the language of rights. Instead, it may involve advocacy on a number of fronts, including reform of corrupt or ineffectual state-controlled food distribution, an end to price supports that make food more expensive, rethinking of agricultural methods that privilege high yield over sustainability, and regulation of global economic forces that raise prices and reduce the supply of food in poorer countries. These are complex policy questions, and all of them involve difficult trade-offs and risk unintended consequences. It doesn't help much to say that there's a right to food, or even that a particular state has a duty to guarantee a right to food, without specifying what that state must do to discharge the duty.

Jeremy Bentham insisted: "There is no right which ought not to be maintained so long as it is upon the whole advantageous to the society that it should be maintained, so there is no right which, when the abolition of it is advantageous to society, should not be abolished. To know [which is which] . . . the time at which the question . . . is proposed must be given, and the circumstances under which it is proposed . . . *the right itself must be specifically described* [italics added], not jumbled with an undistinguishable heap of others under . . . vague general terms. . . ."[12] Even if we reject Bentham's unequivocal utilitarianism, we should heed his call for greater precision; in a sense, Hohfeld's detailed approach to the legal interests described as "rights" achieved the precision called for by Bentham.

For Bentham, precision would serve the cause of practical, context-specific evaluation, allowing us to know which rights it is advantageous to maintain and which it is advantageous to abolish. Bentham allowed for no universal or timeless rights;

he had no confidence that the rights of one society or one era would well serve another place or time. All rights would be subject to a cool and objective utilitarian evaluation. Of course all of the standard objections to utilitarianism apply here. How do we measure overall social utility? Can we somehow weigh the costs of slavery to the enslaved against the benefits to their masters, or the costs to a tortured terrorism suspect against the benefits to the potential victims of terrorism? Still, Bentham's observations serve as a useful counterpoint to the strident absolutism typical of rights assertion, even if we don't embrace his equally strident utilitarianism. At their worst, human rights mandate an overly confident, one-size-fits-all approach to social problems that demand delicate and complex approaches and wrenching policy trade-offs. As human rights activism moves beyond condemning relatively stark and discrete violations—such as genocide, torture, and imprisonment of dissidents—the risk of unintended consequences, the volatility of politics, and the complexities of administration loom larger.

I do not mean to suggest that human rights activists ignore practical challenges to implementation; to the contrary, they are often extremely beady-eyed in advancing their agenda, working strategically to cajole, pressure, and coax reluctant states into compliance. But too often this pragmatic approach is limited to how best to advance some settled human rights principle, one that itself is taken as given, immune from pragmatic evaluation. As law professor and human rights scholar David Kennedy notes, "Human rights activists are proud of their . . . street smarts about what governments are really like, their clever insinuations into the halls of power—but these remain secondary to . . . normative judgment . . . the humanitarian . . . assesses costs and benefits [but only] . . . *for his commitments* . . . he carries no general brief for the social consequences of his initiatives."[13]

The possibility that the human rights principle itself may be counterproductive or ill-suited to a given social milieu is ruled out in advance by the idea that human rights are universal in their application.

It may seem unreasonable to expect human rights activists to engage in a holistic cost-benefit analysis. For the most part, human rights groups are struggling to get negligent and oppressive states just to listen to their concerns. Is there really any risk that we might get "too much" human rights enforcement? Given the woeful level of compliance with humanitarian standards, isn't it safe to assume that any success in human rights enforcement is a good thing?

Not necessarily. It's quite possible that there is too little human rights compliance in some cases and too much enforcement in others. There is, to be sure, widespread violation of many human rights, but human rights groups now play an important role in global governance. They influence the flow of foreign aid, the terms of international trade, the public esteem in which governments are held, and the diplomatic status of nations. They influence national policy and advise heads of states. Today, human rights advocacy is a well-established career path, "human rights" is a respected and sought out domain of expertise, and human rights organizations are thoroughly integrated into an entrenched and remarkably successful project of global governance. Human rights internationalism may not be as influential as the World Wide Web, but it certainly is not as marginal as Esperanto. Human rights groups exercise political power: as much as—and in some cases more than—many government officials.

For the most part, this should be a cause for celebration. Human rights advocacy has grown from a protest movement of questionable significance and esteem—a minor annoyance to despots and tyrants—into a major force in global politics that can undermine regimes and force major changes in national policy. Today, many of the frustrations that the human rights community faces are familiar to anyone exercising power in a federation or decentralized political system: the constant need to cajole inattentive or recalcitrant local leaders, inevitably inconsistent implementation, and unintended consequences due to indigenous influences beyond one's control. But, like a successful professional who still thinks of himself as a countercultural hipster, human rights advocates have retained their youthful identity as scrappy outsiders even as human rights organizations have matured into power brokers on the world stage. This modesty has its charm, but it leads some advocates to underestimate their influence and the responsibility that goes along with it.

Of course it's not fair to hold human rights advocates responsible for every perverse application of human rights, just as it's not fair to hold governments responsible for every unintended consequence of their public policies. And practical impediments to humanitarian goals are no reason to give up on or compromise the highest ideals. But it is fair to ask that human rights groups consider the possibility that some of their advocacy might backfire or ricochet, and to take seriously the concerns of those in the line of fire. And greater realism about the cultural, political, and economic preconditions of humanitarian ends might help define attainable goals and shape practical means for achieving them.

HOW DO RIGHTS AFFECT POLITICAL CONSCIOUSNESS?

In the essay "On the Jewish Question," Karl Marx argued that rights presupposed—and helped to create—a divided self, split between the formally equal, but substantively empty, rights-bearing citizen and the radically distinctive and specific, but isolated and egoistic, rights-bearing individual. Marx wrote: "Man as he is a member of civil society is taken to be the real man, man as distinct from the citizen, since he is man in his sensuous, individual immediate existence, while political man is only the abstract, artificial man, man as allegorical, moral person. Actual man is acknowledged only in the form of the egoistic individual, and the true man only in the form of the abstract citizen."[14] Marx's concern was that rights required a false division of human subjectivity, an alienation from oneself. In order to be integrated into a political community as a rights-bearing equal, one had to ignore or suspend the very things that made one most human—one's passions, cultural distinctiveness, religion, and material needs. Conversely, in order to live as a full, "sensuous" human being, one had to suspend or step outside the domain of political connection and retreat into a circumscribed "private" sphere.

To some extent, rights to cultural distinctiveness, dignified work, health care, and food can be seen as attempts to integrate the political rights-bearing citizen and the "man as he actually is." But, to the extent more expansive human rights address Marx's concerns, they run into the objections raised by Burke and Bentham: Rights to cultural integrity, dignified work, health care, and food cannot be secured by declaration; they require infrastructure, industry, administration, a healthy civil society.

This is why human rights activists now find themselves serving as policy consultants, working with receptive governments on institutional details. But these concerns don't sound in the register of "rights"—at least not as typically conceived. Addressing them will require nurturing and in some cases creating a cosmopolitan political community that will come to consider certain humanitarian goals as a constitutive part of its identity. The growing prestige of human rights suggests that such an aspiration may be realistic, and human rights groups, in what Janet Halley calls their "governance" mode, will be important members of such an emerging community. But Samuel Moyn warns that as human rights groups move into contested political terrain, they inevitably will confront the types of controversies and resistance characteristic of politics generally. Not only will rights not transcend ordinary politics, the abstraction of rights can obscure the details of policy implementation and the absolutism of rights can make needed political compromise harder to accept.

Because rights are more than just a means to end—because they have become an alternative utopian vision—they affect political imagination, shaping and to some extent limiting the kinds of social change that can be envisioned. The individual who puts her faith in "universal" rights may be less likely to find more comprehensive, detailed, and collective political engagement compelling. A telling symptom of this kind of alienated political consciousness is the common slogan that human rights advocates "speak truth to power." This implies that power is always somewhere else and that speaking is not a form of power. Human rights victories from this perspective are not an exercise of power but rather the *negation* of power: Rights keep *other people* from abusing their power. Here, rights are conceived of not as political action but as a reaction to and restraint of politics—as antipolitics. Hence, rights activism can promote an antipolitical conception of engagement.

Despite claims that today's human rights trace their lineage back to such proponents of rights as Thomas Paine, the modern conception of rights assertion without comprehensive political reform is of recent vintage, quite different from that of Paine and his contemporaries. For Paine, natural rights were a justification for political resistance and revolution, not a substitute for them. For instance, in answer to Edmund Burke's attack on the French Revolution and the Rights of Man, Paine insists: "That which a whole nation chooses to do, it has a right to do. . . . I am contending for the rights of the *living*, and against their being willed away, and controlled and contracted for by the manuscript assumed authority of the dead."[15] For Paine, the people have the right to overthrow a government that fails to respect their natural and civil rights—the practical foundation of all rights is the right to change the government. Notice the similarity of this argument in favor of rights to Jeremy Bentham's objection to rights. For Bentham, the menace of rights was that they would become a form of tyranny—a way for the dead to rule from beyond the grave—whereas for Paine the promise of rights was that they were a safeguard against the rule of the dead:

> The circumstances of the world are continually changing, and the opinions of men change also; and as government is for the living, and not for the dead, it is the living only that has any right in it. That which may be thought right and found convenient in one age, may be thought wrong and found inconvenient in another. In such cases, who is to decide, the living, or the dead?[16]

Paine believed that rights superseded and transcended any government—in this sense, rights indeed would be universal.

But most rights could only be exercised collectively. Here Paine distinguishes between natural rights, which inhere in and can be exercised by the individual, and civil rights, which can only be exercised collectively—that is, through government:

> Natural rights are those which appertain to man in right of his existence. . . . Civil rights are those which appertain to man in right of his being a member of society. . . .
>
> The natural rights which he retains are all those in which the Power to execute is as perfect in the individual as the right itself. Among this class, as is before mentioned, are all the intellectual rights, or rights of the mind; consequently religion is one of those rights. The natural rights which are not retained, are all those in which, though the right is perfect in the individual, the power to execute them is defective. They answer not his purpose. A man, by natural right, has a right to judge in his own cause; and so far as the right of the mind is concerned, he never surrenders it. But what availeth it him to judge, if he has not power to redress? He therefore deposits this right in the common stock of society. . . .[17]

Here, the bulk of rights—those that individuals do not have the power to execute themselves—must be guaranteed collectively. This makes the character of collective institutions of the greatest importance. To take Paine's example, since a man cannot provide his own redress, he must allow society to judge his cause and accept society's judgment. This requires a fair and impartial system of adjudication. There is no way of guaranteeing this right without appropriate collective institutions.

Of course, one might imagine that individuals could assert many of Paine's civil rights through international pressure, even when individual governments were inadequate or perverse. But this was not the solution Paine entertained. Instead, Paine envisioned that individual rights would be guaranteed collectively through civil society, and he held that society had the inherent right to "abolish any form of Government it finds inconvenient." Practically speaking, rights were to be asserted collectively, in society, which would work through government when it was just, as in a republic, and which had the right to abolish government when it was unjust, as in a monarchy. For Paine, the important opposition was between government and *society*—not government and the individual. Accordingly, the central concern of his defense of the Rights of Man was not to guarantee rights for the subjects of monarchies or other unjust governments but rather to replace monarchies with republics:

> What we now see in the world, from the Revolutions of America and France, are a renovation of the natural order of things, a system of principles as universal as truth and the existence of man. . . . Monarchical sovereignty, the enemy of mankind, and the source of misery, is abolished; and the sovereignty itself is restored to its natural and original place, the Nation.[18]

Paine believed that just governments would allow the natural cooperative instincts of individuals to flourish, making the respect of rights habitual, while unjust governments would poison social relations between subjects and therefore were incapable of respecting rights. Respect for the Rights of Man was inseparable from political reform:

> The instant the form of Government was changed in France, the republican principles of peace and domestic prosperity and economy arose with the new Government; and the same consequences would follow the cause in other Nations. . . . Instead,

therefore, of exclaiming against the ambition of Kings, the exclamation should be directed against the principle of such Governments; and instead of seeking to reform the individual, the wisdom of a Nation should apply itself to reform the system.[19]

This suggests that when human rights are at odds with the central or organizing ideological commitments of a government, the solution is comprehensive reform or revolution. Take, for instance, the right to equality of the sexes. It's clear that many governments are opposed to a great deal of what most of the world would insist is required by "equal rights for women." For example, Saudi Arabia describes the Sharia principles that mandate a subordinate role for women as the foundation of its government. If equal rights for women are truly universal, then the ultimate ambition of human rights activism must be wholesale reform or the overthrow of such regimes.

Alternatively, universal rights might be limited to those things that are, at least conceptually, compatible with any political system. For instance, one can insist that an autocratic regime not torture its citizens or jail political dissidents; one can demand that a theocracy not persecute atheists and the adherents of minority religions. But this solution leaves us with a fairly short list of potential universal rights; it suggests that human rights advocates must curtail their ambitions and focus only on a few uncontroversial rights. Tellingly, the trend over the past several decades has been just the opposite: the list of human rights has grown to include almost every weighty political, social, and economic issue.

Today's human rights straddle these two approaches: They seek to correct a host of diverse discrete abuses while leaving political systems intact. Indeed, the singular genius of human rights—at least as conceived by organizations such as Amnesty

International and as reflected in such cooperative bodies as the United Nations—is that human rights do not seek to reform any particular political system as such. Human rights stay above the fray of geo-politics and ideological conflict and hence can command the assent of all nations—capitalist and communist, democracy and monarchy, secular republic and theocracy.

But this universality comes at a cost. Today's human rights promote the split political subjectivity that troubled Marx: Rights divide the private interests of the individual from the collective life of the citizen. Instead of collective engagement in society and against oppressive governments, universal rights can encourage a flight from society. Conceptually and intellectually, rights can shift energy away from thinking through practical political and institutional reform and into an idealized domain in which vital interests are defined by legal abstractions. Also, practically, rights shift efforts away from collective engagement in comprehensive change and toward attracting the attention of international legal tribunals and humanitarian organizations.

At times, human rights work hints at a comprehensive ideology, but for the most part it shies away from anything resembling a specific political program, in keeping with its universal aspirations. As a result, however, human rights work tends to be piecemeal—it facilitates discrete demands without an account of the worldview underlying those demands or of the political, economic, and institutional conditions necessary to bring them about. As human rights activism becomes the default utopianism of a generation, the result is an oddly truncated political consciousness—one that can demand women's rights but tolerate patriarchal theocracies, or that can insist on rights to cultural self-determination but condemn the actual practices of many specific cultures. In a sense, the belief that these varied aspirations *could* be compatible reflects the kind of alienation Marx identified with respect to "bourgeois rights" on a potentially global scale: The assertion of rights takes place in isolation from the ideological commitments, political institutions, and social relationships that could make them meaningful.

Of course, sometimes this is the best one can hope for. When faced with an implacable and oppressive regime, universal human rights might be the only way to prevent or limit the worst and most stark abuses. But perhaps this suggests that only the most stark and discrete abuses are matters of universal human rights, while problems with more diffuse and complex causes are better understood as political questions, better taken up through social mobilization and better addressed through more comprehensive institutional reform.

CAN TOO MANY RIGHTS MAKE A WRONG? THE RISKS OF OVERUSE

Rights can maintain their special status as inviolable only if they are limited to cases in which most people are genuinely willing to ignore countervailing considerations. But many of the things now described as human rights *must* be weighed against countervailing concerns and competing claims. When we use the language of rights to press contestable political claims, we encourage the idea that rights must be balanced against other competing and inconsistent claims. Once we get used to treating rights as just one claim among many, it becomes easier to yield to considerations of expediency every time.

For instance, many people, including former US Department of Justice lawyer John Yoo and Associate Justice of the Supreme

Court Antonin Scalia, believe that even the basic human rights against torture should yield to expediency when the stakes are high enough. "What if," Yoo asks rhetorically, "a high-level terrorist leader is caught who knows the location of a nuclear weapon?"[20] Similarly, during a public lecture in Canada, Justice Scalia cited a fictional television counterterrorism agent who regularly faces ticking bombs and cagey terrorists in defense of an expedient approach to human rights: "Jack Bauer [tortured a suspect and as a result] saved Los Angeles. . . . Are you going to convict Jack Bauer?"

Once you make an exception in such an extreme case, it's hard to maintain the integrity of the right in the face of less extreme but still compelling cases. And if you are willing to balance the right against other interests in numerous compelling cases, it's hard to understand why you wouldn't weigh costs and benefits in *every* case. If an imminent threat like a ticking bomb justifies torture, what about a less imminent but still certain threat? If we could avoid a costly and risky military expedition in which many lives would be lost with information gained by torturing a prisoner, wouldn't that be justified too? And if avoiding a certain threat justifies torture, how about a substantial risk? One moves from Jack Bauer to John Yoo pretty quickly. Making exceptions, even in high-stakes cases, suggests that the right in question is just another policy goal, to be weighed in a utilitarian balance with other conflicting goals. If so, there's no reason not to balance rights against convenience and expediency every time.

In this state of affairs, it is not surprising that the United States could manufacture ambiguity and elbow out room for debate about even the most basic and fundamental of human rights: the right of prisoners against torture. After suffering the terrorist attacks of September 11, 2001. most Americans and most people throughout the world agreed that a strong reaction was not only justified but also required. Instead of a strong but measured, targeted, and humane response to the attacks, however, the United States has something between a panic attack and a hissy fit, striking out with its unrivaled military, economic, and political influence indiscriminately and disproportionately. Two wars and thousands of innocent lives later, to our shame, we still cannot simply and firmly acknowledge that it is unacceptable to torture prisoners for information. Instead, even justices of our highest courts have become captivated by perverse and vindictive Hollywood-peddled fantasies of uncompromising antiterrorist agents pummeling recalcitrant terrorists into revealing the location of an armed bomb. If there is any place where the moral conviction and utopian imagination of human rights should carry the day, it is here. Isn't it against precisely these sorts of ignoble impulses that the tradition of human rights should fortify us?

The most well-established human rights tradition teaches us that Yoo and Scalia are wrong about torture; some things shouldn't be subject to cost-benefit calculation. Opposition to torture should and often does transcend political and ideological divides. Some of the more thoughtful conservative thinkers, such as Charles Fried, a Harvard Law School professor and former solicitor general, have expressed vigorous opposition to torture.[21] Is it possible that the laudable attempt to harness the power of human rights to a large and growing number of worthy but vexed and complex causes has left us without the torque needed to push back against the simplest and starkest abuses? When nations in which half the population starves can claim to guarantee a right to food, and nations where women are denied equality in marriage, inheritance, mobility, and personal expression can claim to respect the equality of the sexes, should it surprise us that a country that humiliates and tortures people in its custody can nevertheless claim to respect the rights of prisoners?

PART TWO

Rights in Practice

C alabria is the long, pointy toe of the Italian "boot." It was never a part of the Grand Tour taken by wealthy English and American young men as part of their classical education in the eighteenth century, and it's not prominently featured in tourist books today. Most non-Italians know of Calabria from the side of a bottle: roughly one-fourth of Italian olive oil comes from this heavily agricultural region. Calabria is not the prosaic rural Italy of undulating vineyards, sandstone villas, conifer-lined gravel paths, and small family farmers lovingly tending their heirloom crops. It's the home of Italian industrial agriculture, which, like industrial agriculture in central California or Central America, involves heavy machinery, chemical fertilizers, factory livestock management, and cheap migrant labor—less Frances Mayes than Archer Daniels Midland.

Low-wage farm laborers in the United States come across the Rio Grande from Mexico and Central America; in Italy they come across the Mediterranean Sea from Africa. Undocumented migration from Africa to Italy has become a conspicuous fact of life in recent decades, a disconcerting change for a nation that has long been an embarkation point for immigrants rather than a destination. African men sell small models of Italian landmarks and shirts bearing *il tricolore* outside the Trevi Fountain and the Coliseum in Rome, the Duomo in Milan, and the Bargello Museum in Florence; African women care for the children or ailing parents of the Italian *borghesia* in the prosperous north, and some join desperate migrants from Eastern Europe and Turkey as call girls and streetwalkers in the tougher neighborhoods of Italy's cities. But in agricultural Calabria, undocumented immigrants are not just domestic help or hustlers in the gray market or service sector; they are a vital part of the region's core economy. They harvest crops and work on construction sites in industries dominated by the *Ndrangheta*—the Calabrian Mafia—accepting what Italian journalist and organized crime expert Roberto Saviano called "peanut wages, slave hours and poor living conditions." Some came to Italy surreptitiously, in the desperate hope of a better life. Others, according to human rights organizations such as the intergovernmental International Organization for Migration, were lured with false promises of legal work, only to find they had paid unscrupulous brokers $10,000 or more for the privilege of working as undocumented aliens for $30 a day and living in an abandoned factory without heat or water. *Time* magazine reports that Calabria's "migrants are managed by a Mafia-run employment system, the *caporalato*, that operates like a 21st century chain gang. . . . 'The farm and factory owners employ the Mafia *caporali* to bring the workers. . . . If they complain, they get killed.'"[1] According to a report from Princeton University, the *Ndrangheta* "controls the agriculture market in Calabria, and much of the rest of the economy as well. . . . an African immigrant's ticket to Italy . . . is a deal with the *Ndrangheta*, a ticket to Calabria . . . and work as a day laborer. . . . this system completely bypasses the immigration and labor laws of Italy. . . ."[2]

Rosarno is a city of sixteen thousand surrounded by orange and clementine groves in southwestern Calabria. By 2010, more than two thousand African immigrants had lived in Rosarno for more than twenty years, harvesting fruit for a living. They had become part of the local community, much as itinerant farmworkers have in agricultural communities throughout the prosperous first world, where market economics and landowner avarice push wages below what citizens will accept. But many Italians resented the influx of immigrants, whom they saw as a threat to Italian culture and unfair competition for increasingly scarce work in a depressed economy. Right-wing organizations described them with predictably intolerant invective. Umberto Bossi, founder of the *Lega Nord*—or Northern League—suggested that police open fire on boats carrying African immigrants to Italy. Many of Rosarno's Italians, for their part, "felt disgust at the 'dirty' communities living on the edge of their town,"[3] and some were poor enough to covet even the meager wages and scanty charitable aid the immigrant farmworkers received.

When African immigrants rioted in Rosarno in early January 2010, the backstory seemed to fit a familiar pattern: widespread racism, exploitation, and contempt eventually provoked an understandable if counterproductive reaction. Like Watts in 1964, Detroit in 1967, Los Angeles in 1992, and Paris in 2005, Rosarno had suffered a classic race riot. As is typical, it was hard to identify the cause of the blaze, but once the fire was lit, it found plenty of fuel. On Thursday, January 7, a group of Italian boys shot an African man with an air rifle, injuring his leg. Among the African community, the rumor spread that the gang had shot and killed the man. In frustration, the Africans took to the streets to protest. Later, a rumor spread among Italians that rioting Africans had attacked a pregnant Italian woman in misguided retaliation, killing her baby. This was also untrue, but it provoked a violent backlash. The rioting quickly engulfed the entire town of Rosarno and lasted for two days, as immigrants attacked cars, set fire to trash bins, and smashed windows.

By Saturday, anger was widespread and tension was ubiquitous. Locals insisted that the immigrants had "destroyed" their town, and some were looking for payback. Italian officials began to evacuate the immigrants for their own safety. More than a thousand immigrants either left voluntarily or were escorted out of the Rosarno area and taken to holding centers, where those without proper documentation were processed for deportation. By Sunday, the fire brigade had started to destroy the shantytowns where the immigrants had lived.

The Rosarno rioting focused attention on a host of human rights violations: human trafficking, inhumane working conditions, unfair wages, substandard housing, racial discrimination, and mass deportations arguably motivated by racial animus. Italian politician Luigi Manconi noted, ruefully, that Rosarno after the riots had become "the only wholly white town in the world. Not even South African apartheid obtained such a result." Italy's *La Repubblica* newspaper compared the attacks on immigrants to Ku Klux Klan violence in the United States during the Jim Crow era.[4] The United Kingdom's *Guardian* newspaper described the removal of Rosarno's Africans as "ethnic cleansing."[5]

Human rights organizations condemned the mass detention and deportation of the immigrants, and some complained of bias in law enforcement. A month after the riots, Human Rights Watch noted that authorities had already convicted five migrants but only three Italians had been arrested and none charged.[6] Prosecutors blamed *omertà*—a local culture that discourages cooperation with law enforcement—for their failure to make charges stick against the locals. But the problem may have been more widespread: Prime Minister Silvio Berlusconi's government focused "more on irregular immigration . . . than on the victims" according to Human Rights Watch. In fact, Berlusconi insisted that "a reduction in the number of foreigners in

Italy means fewer people to swell the ranks of criminals"; while Interior Minister Roberto Maroni blamed "the wrong kind of tolerance" for creating the conditions that led to the riots.[7]

Although many Italians were alarmed by these statements, few were surprised. Berlusconi—a conservative multimillionaire industrialist-turned-politician—had formed a governing coalition with the far right *Lega Nord*, of which Roberto Maroni was a member. The *Lega Nord* had advanced a host of alarming, anti-immigrant policy proposals, including bans on foreign cuisine and the construction of mosques and—in an unintentional nod to the Jim Crow laws of the American South—the segregation of immigrants from native Italians on public transportation. A *Lega Nord*–dominated city council in Coccaglio, a town of seven thousand residents (including fifteen hundred immigrants), instituted a two-month sweep to identify and drive out undocumented foreigners. The sweep, which was slated to end on December 25, was informally called *Natale Bianco* (White Christmas). "For me, Chistmas isn't the celebration of hospitality, but rather of Christian tradition and our identity," explained a *Lega Nord* councilor.[8]

All of this made it easy to attribute the violence in Rosarno to racism: the racism of the local residents who shunned, exploited, and attacked the migrants, provoking them to lash out in protest, and the racism of government officials whose anti-immigrant policies left migrants vulnerable to exploitation and who responded to the inevitable clashes by blaming the victim. This diagnosis suggests that the tragedy in Rosarno is the result of a discriminatory state and a prejudiced majority population: a classic human rights violation. And from that it seems to follow that the government and perhaps a few powerful private actors could improve the situation fairly readily.

But there are a few problems with this diagnosis. Although

racism is unquestionably a problem in Italy, the worst offenders seem to be in the industrialized North—not in the agricultural South. The *Lega Nord* came into being as a secessionist group that sought to split prosperous northern Italy from the economically struggling South. The *Lega Nord*'s supporters occasionally even evoked a racial hierarchy that divided Italians: Northern Italians were said to be of a distinct racial stock (more akin to neighboring Austria and France) from the darker southerners, with their Greek, Maltese, and North African influences. Indeed, some derisively referred to southern Italians as "Moroccans." Despite harsh working conditions in the South, African migrants reported more hospitable treatment in southern Italy than in the North: "They actually live better down there than in Milan . . . the human relationships are warmer . . . Africans say the Italian girls look them in the eyes in Calabria, while in the north they wouldn't," reports Roberto Saviano.[9] Immigrants shopped in local stores and had generally amicable relations with the Italians. Before the rioting, many locals in Rosarno had tried to help the immigrants, and most others were quietly resigned to their presence.

Quiet resignation is, by most accounts, the predominant mood in Calabria. Centuries of autocratic rule, foreign domination, patronage, and Mafia overlordism have created a local culture of learned helplessness. Calabria is one of Italy's poorest regions, and, according to political scientist Robert Putnam, it also has the most dysfunctional political institutions and the least vibrant civic culture in Italy. Calabrians do not trust government—and for good reason—nor do they trust each other. Lacking the local institutions and social norms that inspire mutuality and a sense of the common good, Calabrians rely on patronage relationships with powerful elites (or crime bosses) and familial ties. Putnam cites a popular Calabrian proverb: *Chi ara diritto, muore disperato,* or

"He who behaves honestly comes to a miserable end." Another advises, "When you see the house of your neighbor on fire, carry water to your own."[10]

This—the infamous *omertà*—explains why law enforcement has had little success in prosecuting those responsible for the attacks that provoked the Rosarno rioting. Calabrians didn't want to "get involved" with law enforcement, and most feared the *'Ndrangheta*. According to Saviano, the Rosarno riots were not a racial conflict between immigrants and native Italians; they were a rare uprising against the criminal organizations that control much of the agricultural economy of Calabria:

> The riots were widely portrayed as clashes between immigrants and native Italians, but they were really a revolt against the *'Ndrangheta*. . . . everything—jobs, wages, housing—is controlled by criminal organizations. . . . The mafias let the African immigrants live and work in their territories because they make a profit off them. The mafias exploit them. . . . [b]ut they came to make a better life for themselves—and they're not about to let anyone take the possibility of that life away. There are native Italians who reject mafia rule as well, but they have the means and the freedom to leave places like Rosarno. . . . The Africans can't. They have to stand up to the clans."[11]

And Saviano hints at worse to come: "The majority [of immigrants] came to Italy to better themselves, not to be mobsters. But if the Africans in Rosarno had been organized at a criminal level, they would have had a way to negotiate with the Calabrian Mafia. . . . They wouldn't have had to riot."

Ultimately we have a failure of criminal-law enforcement as much as a human rights violation. The Italian government has been engaged in anti-Mafia campaigns for decades, with limited success. The Mafias bribe and intimidate police, judges, witnesses, and politicians, and they easily retool even after setbacks. Calabria's *'Ndrangheta* is widely believed to be the largest and most influential criminal organization in Italy—having eclipsed the more famous Sicilian *Cosa Nostra* and Neapolitan *Cammora*. The *'Ndrangheta* is now a global enterprise, "capable of penetrating anywhere, from Europe to the U.S., from Canada to Australia," according to Francesco Forgione, former president of the anti-Mafia commission of the Italian Parliament.[12] Rather than a race war between natives and immigrants, the riots in Rosarno were a fight between a highly organized multinational criminal gang and its victims who dared to fight back.

Calabria lacked the civic habits and institutions that could have made human rights a viable indigenous commitment. Many Italians lamented the conditions suffered by immigrants in Calabria, but the local population didn't have the civic resources to do anything about it. The *'Ndrangheta* operates with relative impunity and, according to many observers, virtually controls the region's economy. Many Calabrians hate the influence of criminal gangs, but they've lost hope of eliminating or even undermining them. Or, perhaps more accurately, they never had such hope. Putnam traces the civic history of the Mezzogiorno—the southern part of Italy that includes Calabria—back to the eleventh-century Norman Conquest, which brought the cities of southern Italy under strict autocratic rule and established "a steep social hierarchy . . . dominated by a landed aristocracy endowed with feudal powers, while at the bottom masses of peasants struggled wretchedly close to the limits of physical survival. Between . . . cowered a small, largely impotent middle class of administrators and professionals. . . . [for] the next seven centuries . . . this hierarchic structure would endure essentially unchanged."[13]

This durable social hierarchy encouraged patron-client relationships of dependency and punished attempts at self-sufficiency and cooperation for mutual advantage among the common people. According to Putnam:

> political cunning and social connections have long been essential to survival in this melancholy land. . . . The southerner— whether peasant or city-dweller, whether in the old Hapsburg kingdom of the sixteenth century, the new Italian kingdom of the nineteenth century, or . . . the regional politics of the late twentieth century—has sought refuge in vertical bonds of patronage and clientelism. . . . The southern feudal nobility . . . used private violence, as well as their privileged access to state resources, to reinforce vertical relations of dominion and personal dependency and to discourage horizontal solidarity. . . . For wretchedly vulnerable peasants . . . the patron-client system . . . [was] a rational strategy for survival—even when those who are dependent recognize its drawbacks.[14]

Italians in the Mezzogiorno occasionally rebelled against the social hierarchy, adds Putnam, but they were unable to develop lasting organizations or relationships of social solidarity. Instead, rebellion took the form of "[v]iolent protest movements [and] chronic brigandage" and inevitably settled into "the more usual passive reaction of resigned submission. . . . this submission . . . provides the historical background to the acceptance of the arrogation of power by . . . the *mafiosi.*"

The rule of law—including respect for human rights—requires more than a willing government; it requires an engaged and committed citizenry. The great French political theorist Alexis de Tocqueville made this point in contrasting the civic virtues of nineteenth-century America, where "every one is personally interested in enforcing the obedience of the whole community to the law [and] . . . the citizen complies . . . because . . . he regards it as a contract to which he himself is a party," with the lack thereof among some less civic nations—including his native France—where the citizen "cower[s] . . . before the pettiest officer; but . . . braves the law with the spirit of a conquered foe, as soon as its superior force is withdrawn: he perpetually oscillates between servitude and license."[15] The police can't be everywhere and the courts can handle only so much litigation. Every diligent student of the law understands that effective laws work not because of comprehensive surveillance and enforcement but because of widespread acceptance.

When citizens lack the civic ties that allow strangers to trust one another and treat one another honestly, only the ties of blood and patronage remain: the rule of law yields to the rule of men. Perhaps the most chilling observation in Putnam's account of the Mezzogiorno is that the vacuum of civic trust among citizens was filled by "Mafia enforcers [who ensured] . . . that . . . agreements would be kept. 'The most specific activity of Mafiosi [is to] produce and sell trust.' "[16] In a society where social trust and respect for government are so lacking that contracts typically are enforced by the Mafia, the law has essentially stopped working. What would it mean in such a context to speak of human rights violations?

Rights require a relationship of mutual respect and obligation among citizens. In the early twentieth century, legal theorist

Wesley Hohfeld offered an elaborate typology of legal relations to describe what had too-casually been called "rights."[17] Hohfeld argued that rights come in many different forms. Sometimes a "right" involves the legal capacity to do something without interference from others; sometimes it involves the legal capacity to compel the help of others in doing something; sometimes it involves the legal capacity to do something without legal punishment. In each case, the "right" is meaningful only to the extent that it describes a relationship with a specific person, institution, or group. Rights do not describe an asset or a quality held by individuals; they describe a relationship or set of relationships, governed by certain expectations. This understanding of rights isn't exclusive to pointy-headed lawyers and nitpicking skeptics; in fact, one of the most passionate early defenders of rights, Thomas Paine, made a similar, if less detailed, point more than a century earlier than Hohfeld, with respect to Republican France's Declaration of the Rights of Man:

> While the Declaration of Rights was before the National Assembly some of its members remarked that if a declaration of rights were published it should be accompanied by a Declaration of Duties. The observation discovered a mind that reflected, and it only erred by not reflecting far enough. A Declaration of Rights is, by reciprocity, a Declaration of Duties also. Whatever is my right as a man is also the right of another; and it becomes my duty to guarantee as well as to possess.[18]

Paine's conception of rights necessarily implies a social relationship, defined not only by enumerated entitlements but also by mutual respect and loyalty. Government may be necessary to guarantee human rights, but it is not sufficient; responsible citizens are also indispensable. And in order for citizens to be responsible, they must enjoy the civic culture that allows for and nurtures the habits of civic responsibility. This suggests that a down-to-earth idea of human rights work may entail the arduous and uncertain job of undoing centuries of habitual suspicion and hostility and building organic civic institutions and norms. Without these institutions and norms, it's unrealistic to expect that any right will be respected. Does it help to evoke human rights when the source of the problem is an especially resourceful and elusive criminal gang such as the *'Ndrangheta?* *Of course* criminal gangs violate human rights.

The larger problems include the plight of desperate people for whom even the miserable working conditions of Mafia-controlled migrant farmworkers are an improvement over life in their native countries, and an agricultural industry that relies on exploitable migrant labor worldwide. No single state is responsible for the global conditions that result in the transnational migration of desperate people who are ripe for exploitation. Human rights advocates understand this all too well, which explains why the prescriptions they demand often fall so far short of what is needed to correct the problems they identify. For instance, Human Rights Watch condemned the forcible resettlement of migrants and called on Italy to step up the prosecutions of native Italians involved in the Rosarno rioting. Both sensible demands, but neither can stop the exploitation of migrant labor by the Mafia or prevent similar riots in the future.

Maybe the Italian authorities could have been more aggressive in their efforts to stop the *'Ndrangheta.* Perhaps the Italian government discriminated against African immigrants by ignoring Mafia exploitation in the agricultural sector: "It's obvious they have let the Mafia freely do with the immigrants as they wish," Roberto Saviano complains. Law enforcement is a human rights issue if the government deliberately neglects to protect an unpopular group. But aggressive law enforcement has its humanitarian costs too. Would police infiltration of criminal gangs, surveillance, surprise raids, and mass incarceration count as human rights victories? Are the inevitable invasions of privacy, repression of individual liberty, excessive force, and overzealous prosecution that accompany aggressive law enforcement the necessary costs of securing human rights? Policy makers confront these types of trade-offs on a daily basis, but they seem antithetical to the idealism of human rights work. It's hard to imagine a human rights organization explicitly deciding to trade off political freedom and personal liberty for decent working conditions and racial equality. But these are precisely the kinds of questions people who wield power must ask and answer. When human rights advocates convince governments to change their policies and priorities, they are wielding power, so they need to ask these questions too.

Aggressive law enforcement is now one of the main responses to the worldwide human rights violations that accompany transnational migration. The official name for the most disfavored type of migration is *human trafficking*. Human trafficking conjures images of people drugged, captured, and sold into involuntary servitude or slavery, but the working definition includes "the recruitment . . . of a person for labor or services, through the use of . . . fraud. . . ." At least some of the migration from Africa to Italy would qualify as "trafficking" under this definition. Africans were promised legal work at decent wages in Italy, only to find themselves undocumented laborers in industries controlled by gangsters. In theory, Italy could stop trafficking by cracking down on undocumented immigration—a response that would please the *Lega Nord* and other nativists. Of course, in practice this would be very hard to do. Moreover, it wouldn't improve the lives of most of the immigrants now suffering under Mafia-controlled employment. Many immigrants are willing to pay large sums and risk their lives in order to reach prosperous countries like Italy. Ironically, it's possible that we could worsen the lives of such people in the name of respecting their rights.

"Why is your government making our lives difficult?" asked Cindy, a Filipina contract worker living in Japan. Cindy directed her query to Rhacel Salazar Parreñas, an American anthropologist then teaching at UC Davis who was working in a Tokyo nightclub as part of her field research. Cindy was also working as a hostess in a Tokyo club, but she was seeking a more tangible and immediate reward than scholarly enlightenment. She, like thousands of other Filipinas, sought work as a hostess because it offered far better pay than she could earn in the Philippines. Many Filipinas working overseas send most of their earnings home, to help support their families. According to a report of the International Monetary Fund, foreign remittances accounted for a remarkable 9 percent of the Philippines' GDP in 2005.[19]

The plight of Filipina hostesses in Japan is in many ways similar to that of African farm laborers in Italy's Mezzogiorno—both groups seek better opportunities in wealthier nations and both are victims of restrictions on their migration. According to Parreñas, the typical Filipina who wants to work as a hostess in Japan must go through a promotion agency, which arranges an audition with a Japanese promoter who works for a club. The candidates parade in front of the promoter with a number pinned to their chests, like contestants in a low-rent beauty pageant (or cattle at a livestock auction). The promoter chooses the women he wants to hire and arranges for them to emigrate to Japan. He picks up each woman at the airport, delivers her to the club, and takes her back to the airport at the end of her contract. In exchange for these services, the promoter receives roughly $2,000 from the club where the woman is employed—money that is, of course, effectively deducted from her earnings. Unfortunately, the promoter only deals with arrangements in Japan; the contract worker also needs a handler to help her navigate the Philippine bureaucracy for overseas workers and arrange her departure from the Philippines. Migrant workers leaving the Philippines for Japan must obtain a medical clearance, complete predeployment seminars, obtain certification of their artistic skills (in order to qualify for a skilled laborer's visa—never mind that hostesses are selected almost entirely for their physical appearance), and pass an exam demonstrating their knowledge of Japanese language and culture. This isn't easy—or cheap. The seminars, exams, lively-arts training, and passports all come with fees, and the handlers who shepherd the young women through the process (analogies to livestock keep suggesting themselves) may demand half their earnings for the next *six years*. This obligation stands whether or not the woman actually works for six years. She is effectively indentured to her manager; if she quits, she must buy out her contract. Moreover, if she fails to complete her contract with the Japanese club, she must also compensate the promotion agency that arranged the initial audition.

Such contracts may not be legally valid, but neither were many of the contracts that kept black sharecroppers tied to the land in the American South after Reconstruction. This made little difference to the sharecropping system that endured for decades despite its illegality, and it makes little difference today to vulnerable young women without the sophistication or resources to hire lawyers. Like southern plantation owners chasing a runaway, many managers prefer direct coercion and extortion to the courts. They hold the passports of their charges until they leave the Philippines and then hand the documents over to the Japanese promoter or club owner, who keeps them while the women are in Japan.

Why would anyone agree to such terms? Undoubtedly some don't—they are duped or forced. But the women whom Parreñas met in Japan's nightclubs—clubs that catered to wealthy salarymen as well as down-market dives run by the *Yakuza* (Japanese mafia)—entered into their contracts voluntarily and with eyes open. They understood the terms of engagement and they eagerly sought out the promoters, who turn away many more applicants than they accept. The grim truth is that a job in a Japanese nightclub—even when all of the costs, fees, wage deductions, and unconscionable contract terms are taken into consideration—is better than anything many women can hope to find at home. Hostesses in Japan are relatively well paid; in 2005, the minimum wage for a foreign entertainer was 200,000 yen, or about $1,700 a month. Even though many nightclubs don't pay the minimum wage, and the average wage that Filipina contract workers actually receive is often much less, few complain.

In exchange for her relatively generous wages, a hostess in a Japanese nightclub does a bit more than show customers to their tables and serve drinks. She is sort of a chanteuse–cum–rent-a-date for patrons of the club. She entertains the customers on stage, singing and dancing. She also engages the customers at their tables, striking up charming and witty conversation, flirting, pouring drinks, lighting cigarettes, even feeding the customers. Some also have to play the role of sexual conquest: flirting, massaging, fondling, allowing herself to be fondled, feigning sexual attraction. Typically, she is not required to have sex with the customers—a hostess is not a prostitute. But some hostesses do sleep with some of the clientele, making it even harder for those who don't want sex to draw the line between the role playing that is part of the job and unwanted physical intimacy.

Worse, they may be pressured to sleep with clients. For instance, one woman Parreñas interviewed, whom she called "Kay," had four regular customers, each of whom considered himself her "boyfriend." Each of these men frequented the bar to see this woman, brought gifts, bought drinks, and left big tips in anticipation of sexual rewards. Kay knew the score; her job was to deliberately encourage these men and keep them coming back to the club. Her boss didn't care whether or not she slept with any of them—provided they kept coming back. But Kay had no intention of sleeping with any of them—she found them all unattractive and refused to become a prostitute. Instead, she hoped to string them along with vague implied promises of something more in the future. Of course, the "boyfriends" began to get impatient. Kay's boss at the club told her she would be invited back for a second six-month contract only if she kept a regular customer happy—she had better sleep with at least one of them. If her clients quit coming in, the club would drop her. This would mean another audition back in the Philippines, additional expenses, and the need to start at the bottom in a new club.

Parreñas's account of the life of a hostess in a down-market Japanese bar reveals an appalling and exploitative employment relationship. But it doesn't jibe with the view of many feminists and human rights activists who describe these hostesses as victims of human trafficking and sexual slavery. These women are "trafficked" in the sense that other people make money by arranging their migration—they are used as objects of commerce. No doubt some hostesses succumb to the pressure to sleep with customers. And their situation—alone and in a for-

eign country, without their passports and trapped in an indentured relationship with their managers—could be described as
a form of slavery. But the women Parreñas interviewed were
not tricked or coerced—they sought out and competed for jobs
and willingly paid to leave their homes and travel to Japan.
Some, like Kay, proved to be savvy—if desperate—entrepreneurs
engaged in a delicate and high-stakes gamble. Their situation is
not enviable, but the language of trafficking and slavery doesn't
capture its distinctive indignities; instead, that language empha-
sizes some of the perils these women can face (those associated
with unwanted sex) and ignores other, arguably more serious
harms (the exploitation that accompanies transnational migration). In fact, describing the plight of these unfortunate women
in the human rights terms of trafficking and sexual slavery
might even *contribute* to their exploitation.

The United Nations Protocol to Prevent, Suppress and Punish
Trafficking in Persons, Especially Women and Children seeks
to end

> the recruitment, transportation, transfer, harbouring or receipt
> of persons, by means of the threat or use of force or other
> forms of coercion, of abduction, of fraud, of deception, of the
> abuse of power or of a position of vulnerability or of the giving
> or receiving of payments or benefits to achieve the consent of
> a person having control over another person, for the purpose
> of exploitation.[20]

The protocol—a supplement to the United Nations Convention
against Transnational Organized Crime—was the result of years
of lobbying and negotiation by human rights groups, feminists,

and national governments. It reflected compromise among constituencies with diverging views when possible and an expedient ambiguity—an agreement to disagree—when it was not. For instance, feminists were split as to whether their ultimate goal should be the abolition of prostitution or reforms to ensure that women had free choice and better working conditions. Feminists who favored abolition found common cause with religious conservatives—especially Christians in the United States—who supported ratification of the protocol and assertive parallel legislation in the US Congress in order to promote conservative sexual morality.[21] Although many feminists around the world believed that abolition of prostitution was unrealistic and would harm women engaged in sex work, in the United States those who questioned abolition were treated with contempt by both Left and Right. For instance, when the Clinton administration supported including *forced* prostitution but not other types of prostitution in the definition of "sexual exploitation"—hence allowing for the possibility of consent to prostitution—the National Organization for Women, the Planned Parenthood Federation of America, and noted feminists such as Gloria Steinem complained of an "effort to weaken international laws against the trafficking of women and children for prostitution."[22] Meanwhile, conservative organizations such as the Heritage Foundation attacked the administration's position in similar terms, derided the group working on antitrafficking—the President's Interagency Council on Women—as a "hooker panel," and accused the administration of "shrugging its shoulders" at sex trafficking.[23]

For the United States, sex trafficking was a law-enforcement problem as much as it was a human rights violation. The Clinton administration's work on sex trafficking grew out of its anti-crime initiatives focusing on the drug trade, money laundering, illegal immigration, and "piracy" (violations of intellectual property such as counterfeit brand-name goods, bootleg DVDs, and pharmaceuticals made in violation of corporate patents). Sex trafficking fit nicely into an agenda that already treated porous national borders as portals for vice and theft. Although the Clinton administration did not adopt the abolitionist position on trafficking, its law-enforcement approach lent itself to a hard line. The administration's efforts resulted in the Trafficking Victims Protection Act of 2000 (TVPA), which, among other things, makes anti-trafficking policies a condition of U.S. foreign aid. The TVPA requires the State Department to monitor the antitrafficking efforts of foreign governments receiving aid from the United States and submit annual Trafficking in Persons (TIP) Reports to Congress. The reports detail the shortcomings of each nation's antitrafficking laws and assign an overall grade: Tier 1, Tier 2, and Tier 3. A country that sinks to Tier 3 risks the suspension of all nonhumanitarian and nontrade–related aid.

The 2004 TIP Report warned of the "Abuse of 'Artistic' or 'Entertainer' Visas" by traffickers to bring victims into Japan. According to the report, "Japan issued 55,000 entertainer visas to women from the Philippines in 2003, many of whom are suspected of having become trafficking victims." It suggested that "[a]uthorities should scrutinize the requirements for issuing these types of visas and implement screening procedures. . . ."[24] The report placed Japan on the Tier 2 Watch List, admonishing that "Japan's trafficking problem is large . . . the Japanese Government must begin to fully employ its resources to address this serious human rights crime within its borders." The report threatened that Japan's "placement on the Tier 2 Watch List is based on its commitments to bring itself into compliance with the minimum standards by taking additional steps over the next year." Among the efforts of other nations that the report praised were: "[t]ighter 'entertainer' visa issues and control procedures . . . for nationals from Colombia, a major source of trafficking victims."[25]

Japan took the hint. In 2005, the TIP Report noted, approvingly, that the Japanese "government . . . took major steps to significantly tighten the issuance of 'entertainer visas' to women from the Philippines," and in 2006 the report noted "remarkable progress in the government's efforts to tighten the issuance of 'entertainer visas' to Philippine nationals. . . ." Most of Japan's other antitrafficking measures were insignificant or ineffective. For instance, the government contributed only about $100,000 to shelters for trafficking victims. The 2008 TIP Report noted that, "although victims were eligible for special stay status as a legal alternative to repatriation in cases where victims would face hardship or retribution . . . most victims were unaware they could extend this status or apply for a change of status to one that permits employment. . . . there has never been a case of a victim staying in Japan for more than a few months."

The Japanese government's main response to trafficking was to seal its borders. If the goal is abolition of prostitution above all else, perhaps this is progress. Less migration probably means less trafficking. In this respect, however, one notes with some unease a 2008 TIP Report finding that "a significant number of Japanese men continue to travel to other Asian countries, particularly the Philippines . . . to engage in sex. . . ." Could the crackdown on trafficking from the Philippines to Japan be related to increased sex tourism from Japan to the Philippines? But it requires a big leap of faith, propelled by a muscular paternalism, to arrive at the conclusion that sealed borders are good for the women who sought out jobs as hostesses in Japan, aware of the risks and downsides. No one would argue that these women are happy with the terms of their employment, but many prefer

it to the available alternatives. For instance, the woman Parreñas called "Kay" was determined that she would not sleep with
men she neither liked nor found attractive, but she did not seek
escape; instead, she hoped to string her clients along. Kay did
not fear unwanted sex as much as the prospect of *losing her job
as a hostess*. And if she did lose her job, she planned to "parad[e]
herself once again in front of a promoter in the Philippines to
secure yet another six-month contract to entertain men. . . ."[26]

Of course it's possible that Kay and the other women Parreñas
interviewed were lying, deluded, or so psychologically damaged
that they accepted or even eroticized their own domination and
subjugation. It's tempting to insist that no one could ever willingly make such a choice, that all sex workers—whether prostitutes or those like Kay who work in the ambiguous territory
between hospitality and prostitution—must have been coerced.
In the United States, feminism and conservative religious morality combined to unequivocally condemn sex work and malign
the people who claim to have chosen it. Two powerful—and typically opposed—political constituencies came together in support
of the idea that sex work *by its very nature* violates human rights.
For instance, the Bush administration, at the urging of religious
conservatives, used the Trafficking Victims Protection Act to
press for the abolition of prostitution.[27] When the TVPA was
reauthorized in 2003 under President Bush, it required organizations seeking US antitrafficking funds to pledge in their grant
applications that they did not "promote, support or advocate
the legalization or practice of prostitution."[28] The Bush administration imposed the same condition on groups receiving AIDS-
prevention funds, resulting in what Indian legal scholar Prabha
Kotiswaran has called a "Cold War sensibility, where sharp
lines are drawn between those who want to abolish sex work
. . . and those who are more ambivalent. . . . NGOs perceived

to advocate the legalization of sex work have been visited with swift sanctions through the loss of international funding. . . . sex worker organizations are being starved of their already limited funds, while . . . international outposts of U.S. church-based organizations are flush. . . ."[29]

Some feminists insist that sex work is intrinsically exploitative and coercive, but others allow for the possibility that some women might consent to engage in sex work. Still others argue that labor markets for sex work are not inherently different from other labor markets, and they insist that workers are exploited when they lack the ability to organize or face constraints on their mobility.[30] Sex-workers' unions, pro-sex feminists, pragmatic liberal feminists, and doctors engaged in disease prevention have allied against universal prohibition and in favor of context-specific policies designed to help women make the best of their existing circumstances. When an organization distributes condoms or advocates other policies that would protect prostitutes from disease, violence, and coercion, has it "supported the practice of prostitution"? One needn't favor the legalization of prostitution to have doubts about the wisdom of the Bush administration's policy of universal prohibition, just as one needn't think cocaine should be available for sale at the corner store to question the wisdom of America's long and costly War on Drugs. Yet, refracted and intensified by the lens of American radical feminism and Christian moralism, human rights have become a powerful rationale and tool for a "zero-tolerance" approach to the world's oldest profession.

The human rights approach to the varied and complex problems that now fall under the ambiguous label of "sex trafficking" has encouraged us to believe that the worst injury these women suffer is *sexual*. But perhaps these women are not victims of unwanted sex as much as they are victims of restrictive immigration policies. Parreñas's account depicts savvy—indeed, world-weary—young women who make informed decisions about what they are willing to do and who know what to expect in return. "Kay" drew the line at sex with her customers. No doubt many women eventually relent and consent to sex, and others are forced into prostitution by club owners, *Yakuza* mob bosses, or customers who lure them out of the relative safety of the nightclub. In theory, a hostess who is pressured to have sex with customers can quit, notify the police, and return home. But in many cases her promoter in Japan will insist on a penalty if the hostess wants to leave without fulfilling her contract, and the club owner or promoter may retain her passport and visa as "security" to prevent her from leaving without settling her debts. The choice to return home is especially unattractive if she is locked into a long-term relationship with a manager in the Philippines and must either work for six years or pay an exorbitant penalty to buy out her contract. A hostess who doesn't attract a regular group of admirers will not be invited back after her contract expires. She faces a choice: How far will she go to keep her job and avoid another cattle call, possibly ending in a less desirable job or no job at all? These problems are the result of immigration restrictions, not sex work per se, and certainly not the transnational mobility that trafficking restrictions impede.

Let me emphasize that even under the best of circumstances these are difficult, demeaning, and exploitative jobs, and we should all work to create a world in which no one would feel the need to accept them. But are they worse than, say, jobs mining coal, where workers endure exposure to toxins and the ever-present risk of explosions and cave-ins; or jobs harvesting agriculture, where workers often suffer exposure to toxic pesticides, backbreaking labor crouched under netting, and unsanitary

lodging; or jobs in the military, where soldiers risk disfigure-
ment, permanent psychological trauma, and death? We accept
that rational people choose these and many other unpleasant
and dangerous jobs, so perhaps we should also accept the decisions of poor women with few opportunities at home to choose
unpleasant work abroad on the margins of the sex trade.

Most important, notice how the *details* of the employment
relationship—not the nature of the work itself—make the difference between tolerable if unpleasant work and exploitation. A
host of laws, policies, and practices conspire to make women
such as "Kay" vulnerable to exploitation. They are victims of
a weak position in the employment market—a position made
even weaker by the parasitic brokers, agents, and middlemen
with whom they are forced to deal. If women seeking jobs as
hostesses could simply negotiate directly with their employers,
rather than through intermediaries, they would be able to insist
on more favorable terms of employment and retain much more
of their wages. Like other employees, they could work for as long
as the job was acceptable and quit if it became intolerable. They
could move freely from one job to another—rewarding employers who offer (relatively) humane working conditions and pun-
ishing those who abuse their employees. Of course, criminals
would still threaten and extort money and sexual services from
some women, and even the improved hostess jobs would not be
free of the sexual predation inherent in such transactions. But
the jobs would be better and women would be free to leave the
worst of them and seek the protection of police when threatened
or assaulted.

Ironically, the restrictions ostensibly designed to ensure their
safety often make these women more vulnerable to exploitation
and abuse. The Philippine laws that require Japanese employers
to work through agents in the Philippines rather than negotiat-

ing directly with employees are supposed to ensure that foreign businesses comply with Philippine labor standards, but in practice they require Filipinas seeking work abroad to employ intermediaries, who demand unconscionable commissions and bind them in indentured servitude. Under pressure from the United States, Japan has tightened its requirements for entertainer visas, which the State Department insists were abused by sex traffickers to smuggle their victims across national borders. But tighter requirements have created a maze of regulations that Filipinas seeking jobs in Japan must navigate: more classes, tougher exams, more documentation, and more expense, making these women even more dependent on loan sharks, handlers, and intermediaries in both the Philippines and Japan. These restrictions on transnational mobility may make it harder for criminal traffickers, but they undoubtedly make it harder for needy people in poor countries to find work in wealthier countries.

Human rights groups have focused attention on the plight of abused women worldwide, and human rights have given us a language to describe and condemn practices that contribute their exploitation. But human rights analysis too often suggests a one-size-fits-all approach to a variety of different problems. Treating "sex trafficking" as a violation of universal human rights conflates the plight of women who have been abducted or lured away from their homes under false pretenses—victims of porous borders and sexual predators abroad—with that of women indentured to parasitic go-betweens who stand between them and overseas jobs—victims of restrictive borders and poverty at home. The language of human rights has encouraged criminal prohibition and increased policing of national borders—no doubt helping reduce the number of abducted women but also making matters worse for women seeking better opportunities away from home.

This trade-off may be worth it, but it's hard to be sure because the decision to pursue human rights enforcement is rarely described or analyzed as a trade-off. Instead, too many activists have treated any and all migration for sex work as "trafficking" and a violation of human rights deserving of unequivocal condemnation. Following this lead, national governments celebrate immigration restrictions that bar the entry of potential sex workers (along with many other migrants) as a human rights victory.

Of course, human rights activists didn't demand immigration restrictions—they only insisted that nations had a responsibility to stop trafficking and sexual exploitation. They urged a number of reforms, including allowing the victims of trafficking to stay in countries such as Japan under new visas that would allow them to get decent work. National governments—not human rights groups—have the final say in the details of implementation. But it's no surprise that many governments prefer a crackdown on politically powerless immigrants to tighter regulation or criminal prosecution of their own citizens. Immigration restrictions were a predictable consequence of antitrafficking advocacy. Human rights activism has helped to shape US foreign policy, which in turn has influenced the policies of national governments worldwide. In this sense, human rights activism played an important role in encouraging and justifying the crackdown. And the language of human rights can also be used as a tool of propaganda—to advance political agendas independent of, and even antagonistic to, humanitarian values. For instance, despite its refusal to ratify several important international human rights conventions—including the Convention on the Elimination of All Forms of Discrimination against Women—the United States was happy to wave the banner of women's rights over its antiprostitution agenda.

It is tempting to imagine that the vindication of human rights doesn't involve the messiness of public policy, bureaucracy, law enforcement, and state violence. But human rights advocates are increasingly important players in international diplomacy. They successfully embarrass recalcitrant governments and encourage powerful governments such as the United States to pressure weaker governments to accept reforms. Human rights work is not separate from the public policy of government and public policy is not the exclusive domain of sovereign states. Practically speaking, governance is a complex negotiation among national governments, multinational bodies such as the United Nations, treaty organizations, multinational corporations, the press, and nongovernmental organizations, including human rights groups. Human rights activists are now part of the governing process and thus bear some responsibility for it. Speaking in terms of universal rights can encourage us to ignore the practical details of governance and implementation, the need for tough choices, the inevitable influence of domestic politics, and as an examination of food distribution in India will demonstrate, the limitations and capacities of the local administrative bureaucracies responsible for achieving change on the ground.

Parties to the Universal Declaration of Human Rights and the International Covenant on Economic, Social and Cultural Rights are obliged to guarantee their citizens the right to adequate food. India is a party to both, and its national constitution also guarantees a right to life, which the Indian Supreme Court has interpreted to include a right to food. India is home to a vibrant postindustrial economy that competes with the West in many respects: Europeans and Americans now purchase Indian software engineering, telemarketing, even legal services. A middle-class American buying domestic airline tickets or making a hotel reservation for a weekend in a nearby city may well have her order taken by a better-educated clerk sitting in Bombay. Despite its impressive technological development, however, India is also home to the world's largest concentration of poverty. Three hundred fifty million Indians live on less than one American dollar a day. This is why, despite its technological sophistication and growing middle class, in 2010 India ranked 134th of 182 countries on the United Nations Human Development Index, which measures lifespan, education, and standard of living. Half of India's children are malnourished—a higher fraction than in sub-Saharan Africa.

The juxtaposition of abject poverty alongside high-tech mastery and burgeoning wealth—the stuff of *Slumdog Millionaire*—might be easier to explain if India had relatively little arable land or suffered from primitive agricultural methods. But more than half of the Indian population makes its living from farming, and since the famous Green Revolution of the 1960s and 1970s, Indian farmers have used high-yield seeds and modern irrigation methods to improve harvests—from 50 million tons in the 1950s to 209 million tons in 2000, more than enough to feed everyone in India.[31]

Why hasn't that grain reached India's starving people? If India were exporting food while its people starved—as the British did during the Irish potato famine—perhaps the Indian government would be obliged by its human rights commitments to halt exports and ensure that the food went to the domestic market. But the Indian government banned most exports of wheat and non-basmati rice in 2007. So perhaps human rights obligate the Indian government to purchase and distribute food to its needy citizens directly. But the Indian government has been doing just that since the 1950s. The government purchases huge amounts of grain at artificially inflated rates in order to ensure the economic viability of Indian farmers, and then it sells grain at subsidized rates to the Indian consumer. This system was originally designed primarily as a price support, but in the 1970s it was also charged with providing affordable food for India's poor. India now delivers food through a vast network of regional distributors and local "fair price shops."

Ideally, this system would guarantee local farmers a decent price for their crops and India's poor access to affordable food. In fact, it has led the Indian government to stockpile ever-larger surpluses of grain, which rots as its people starve. In 2002, the government had stockpiled 53 million metric tons of wheat— enough to stretch to the moon and back twice if lined up in bags.[32] Some of this stockpile is a prudent reserve against natural famine, but much of it is left to rot under canvas tarps and in muddy fields. Meanwhile, roughly 350 million Indians go hungry every day. Human rights litigation has prompted increasingly aggressive oversight by the Indian Supreme Court, but by 2010 the reserves had swelled to roughly 60 million metric tons, of which 17.8 million tons were left exposed to the elements, at risk of spoiling in monsoons and becoming infested with insects.[33] Indeed, even as many observers lambasted the Indian government for refusing to export or distribute its surplus in the face of global price inflation, others speculated that "the amount of *edible* wheat in FCI [Food Corporation of India] warehouses is much, much smaller than India's official wheat reserves."[34]

Why was grain left to rot while millions starved? The Indian system of public food distribution suffers from divided motives, incompatible objectives, inefficiency, corruption, and political patronage. Part of the problem is its haphazard nature. The system was originally designed as a price support for farmers and a means of ensuring adequate national reserves against famine and other natural catastrophes—only later was it expanded to distribute subsidized grain and other necessities to the poor.[35] Because the government is such a large buyer, its actions distort the private market. There's little doubt that large purchases of grain at guaranteed prices inflate the price of the remaining grain on the open market, so, by subsidizing farmers through price supports, the government is making it more expensive for its citizens to feed themselves. Of course, there are good reasons to subsidize farmers: India's Green Revolution, which made the subcontinent self-sufficient in terms of its food supply, succeeded in large part by vastly expanding the amount of land used to grow basic staples; without the subsidies, many farmers might decide to shift to cash crops for export or convert their land to other uses, leaving India without adequate staple crops and vulnerable to famine. Nevertheless, the subsidy makes food less affordable and makes the poor even more dependent on the government distribution of food.

Unfortunately, the government supply chain includes several tiers of bureaucracy, offering multiple opportunities for inefficiency, corruption, and theft.[36] The state sets two prices for grain: a heavily subsidized price for families living below the poverty line and a higher price for everyone else. Inaccurate information, red tape, and fraud cause the state to deny many eligible families subsidized grain and allow ineligible families to take advantage of the subsidy. Food allotments also are distorted by regional politics: politically powerful regions get more than they need and powerless regions are left with inadequate supplies.[37] Grain allotments take little account of regional variations in diet; as a result, the poor are offered subsidized grain that they do not know how to use and must resell in order to purchase their traditional staples. Officials in charge of distribution extort bribes from the owners of the "fair price shops" that sell subsidized grain to the poor; to recoup their losses, the shopowners divert subsidized grain to ineligible buyers at market prices. Moneylenders unlawfully take as collateral the ration cards that allow the poor to purchase food at subsidized prices and use them to take advantage of the subsidized price themselves, selling the food on the open market for many times the subsidized price.[38] According to academic studies and the government's own internal evaluations, more than half of the grain meant for the poor is stolen, sold at market prices, or allowed to spoil. One study found that it costs the Indian government six rupees to deliver one rupee's worth of direct aid to the poor.[39]

In response, Indian human rights activists have lobbied the government and sued in court for a "right to food"—a guarantee they insist the Indian government has already accepted under international human rights conventions. No one would argue with the goal of putting more food into the mouths of India's poor, but what is gained by calling this goal a human right? And what, if anything, might be lost by doing so?

Human rights are typically guaranteed by nation-states. Hence, a right to food suggests that government must take charge of the situation and provide the goods directly if private actors fail to do so. The United Nations Right to Food Unit offers a representative analysis:

> Given that adequate food is a human right, what follows? Just as with any other human right . . . what follows is that *states* have certain duties that individuals can justifiably demand that they carry out. States have the obligation to 'respect, protect and fulfil'; that is, first the state must not itself deprive anyone of access to adequate food; second, it must protect everyone from being deprived of such access in any other way; and third, when

anyone is in fact without adequate food *the state must . . . ensure that it is provided.*"[40]

Similarly, Sameer Dossani of Amnesty International insists that "lack of access to services, clean drinking water, adequate education, housing, employment" are "violations of the Universal Declaration of Human Rights and the International Covenant on Economic, Social and Cultural Rights. . . . *it is ultimately the responsibility of governments to end them* . . . [and] ensure that human rights—including the right to live a life of dignity—are respected."[41] In India, this kind of reasoning has led many human rights activists to reject market-based solutions out of hand, in favor of in-kind distribution of food by the state. And if state-controlled distribution is leaving millions starving, then the solution must be to *expand* it and increase public subsidies. For instance, in 2010, when the president of the Indian National Congress Party, Sonia Gandhi, supported a constitutional right to food and a new entitlement to an enlarged public subsidy, the main complaint of many human rights groups was that the reform did not sufficiently increase the government's role.[42]

If government bears the ultimate responsibility for providing food, then a larger role for government in countries like India, where many people are starving, seems to be the only acceptable response. But step back from a conventional human rights perspective and other promising solutions come into view. Many economists believe that India's poor would be better off if the existing system of public support were dismantled in favor of some sort of voucher system or cash subsidy, which would allow poor families to buy the food they need on the open market.[43] They point out that many of India's poor families must purchase their food on the open market despite the huge public distribution system, but because the government is such a large buyer, market prices are higher than they otherwise would be.[44] If government limited its purchases to those necessary to maintain reserves against famine or natural disaster, it would free up a vast supply, resulting in lower market prices for consumers. These economists admit that the distribution of vouchers will be difficult, especially in rural areas without an advanced financial infrastructure. But the complexities of distributing cash, vouchers, or "smart" credit cards to the poor pale in comparison to the complexities of purchasing and distributing food in kind.

In a sense, proposals to replace public distribution of food with market-based antihunger programs repudiate the idea that the government bears the ultimate responsibility for eliminating hunger. A market-based approach, coupled with subsidies that go directly to consumers, tries to leave procurement and administration to private actors, who may have more expertise and better incentives than government. Of course, market forces come with their own unique risks. Farmers who no longer enjoy a guaranteed market for staple crops at a set price might shift to cash crops; subsidies might not match inevitable price fluctuations, leaving the poor with a varying amount of food from month to month; vouchers, food stamps, or cash grants might be vulnerable to their own unique types of graft. Still, it is hard to imagine that any such ills would be either greater or more difficult to cure than those that currently cripple the public system, with its staggering inefficiency. And there is no reason whatsoever to imagine that an *expanded* public system would not be accompanied by a proportionate expansion of theft, graft, and waste.

It seems mean-spirited to suggest that food might not be a human right. Even to suggest that an ambitious human rights guarantee may not be a good idea seems to flirt with callousness. Questioning a new human right inevitably will sound like questioning the substantive goals underlying the right. Edmund Burke's caustic skepticism about positive rights to food and medicine seem like a cruel reactionary's reluctance to feed the hungry and cure the sick. One can almost hear the echoes of Ebenezer Scrooge: "If they would rather die, they had better do it and decrease the surplus population." This sense that rights are synonymous with the goals they seek to guarantee has made rights seem to be equivalent to virtue itself, accounting for much of their prestige and charisma. No one wants to take the side of Scrooge against Bob Cratchit and Tiny Tim.

Most people instinctively believe that human rights should address all of the most important human needs. So we begin by identifying the most dire needs and the most severe injustices and then define a right to meet those needs and end those injustices. But perhaps this is the wrong way to think about rights. There are a lot of important things that aren't (or shouldn't be) the subject of rights and a lot of relatively trivial things that are (and should be). That's because rights are well suited to securing certain things and badly suited to securing others. For instance, compare these two qualities: artistic expression and emotional intimacy. As important as I think it is to write provocative essays, I suspect most people would say that human intimacy is *much* more important. I can imagine living a reasonably fulfilled life that didn't include the freedom to write erotic poetry or politically controversial essays. I can't imagine a reasonably fulfilled life that didn't include friends, family, and lovers. But American law and international law have both developed extensive rights to freedom of expression that extend even to relatively trivial things, such as the ability to write offensive and juvenile parodies of important people and to publish pornography. Yet no one has seriously proposed a positive right to emotional intimacy, even though for most people life would be intolerable without it. Why?

The answer is obvious once one focuses on implementation. Although intimacy is very important, it is impossible to guarantee. Of course, we could (and should) demand that states not interfere with intimate relationships, say, by prohibiting intimacy between mutually consenting adults. But beyond that, how can anyone guarantee cozy candlelit dinners and meaningful conversations to the many lonely hearts that haunt the world? If all people have a right to intimacy, who bears the corresponding obligation? In this case, the most that public policy can do is to help build a social environment that nurtures meaningful relationships. After that, individuals must be left to their own efforts, and it's inevitable that some will fare well and others poorly. Many of the most important things in life, such as intimacy, companionship, meaningful work—and perhaps also things such as food and health care—cannot be guaranteed by rights.

New York University economist William Easterly complains that "some use the word 'human rights violation' to be equivalent to 'extremely bad thing' but . . . there are many different 'extremely bad things,' and it helps if everybody discriminates between them."[45] Many bad things, he suggests, can't be fixed with rights, or well understood in terms of rights. He argues that a useful definition of a human rights violation is one in which we can identify whose rights are being violated and by whom. Only then can activists zero in on the right target and hope to provoke social change:

> The government officers of the slave-owning antebellum US and the slave-owners were violating the rights of slaves—leading to activism against such violators that eventually yielded the

Emancipation Proclamation. The local southern government officers were violating the civil rights of southern blacks under Jim Crow, leading to activism against these violators that yielded the Civil Rights Act and the Voting Rights Act. The apartheid government officers in South Africa violated the rights of black South Africans, and activism against these violators brought the end of apartheid.

In each case Easterly cites, the violator was a state actor, which fits well with the international human rights doctrine that states are the ultimate guarantors of rights. We can imagine a more generous conception of rights, in which some important private actors are also guarantors of rights, but Easterly is right to insist that we need a clear idea of who must guarantee any right, that the party in question must be capable of doing so, and that it must be realistic and just to insist that it do so.

Easterly insists that "poverty does not fit this definition of right . . . calling poverty a human rights violation does not point to any concrete actions that the 'violator' must stop. . . ." Of course, a right to food might suggest some concrete actions a state must *take*. But this returns us to the problem of expertise and administrative competence. Even if India's government *should* ensure that its citizens have food, decades of failure are ample proof that it is incapable of doing so. This may be due to political corruption and compromised motivations, but these are real impediments—much as lack of resources or of technical expertise may be for another government. After all, any government is a collection of institutions, procedures, and warring political forces. Ironically, the very features that make government democratic and responsive to multiple constituencies can also make it unfocused, inefficient, and slow to change. It's easy to blame a highly centralized dictatorship for human rights failures because a discrete entity is in control. By contrast, it's harder to assign responsibility to democratic federations, like India's, that decentralize authority or work through coalition politics. Suppose powerful interest groups ensure that food distribution serves farmers and empowered regions at the expense of starving families in powerless regions. We can call this a human rights violation, but it may be a fairly intractable feature of India's government, a practical constraint on what it can do. India would hardly be unique among democratically governed societies in this respect; the United States and most of Europe set trade and agriculture policy at the behest of powerful political lobbies that insist on trade barriers and demand subsidies that can undermine other important policy goals. Any new effort will have to work through the same political institutions that made reform necessary in the first place. As a result, intensified efforts probably will come with intensified corruption and inefficiency. In these circumstances, the best way to feed India's poor may be to urge the government to do less.

The Convention on the Elimination of All Forms of Discrimination against Women requires signatory nations to "abolish all discriminatory laws and . . . ensure the elimination of all acts of discrimination against women by persons, organizations and enterprises." Unlike a right to food or dignified work, this seems straightforward enough. It is a relatively conventional legal mandate that finds precedent in the domestic civil rights laws of many nations. Unlike a right to be free of trafficking, CEDAW has few ambiguities as to what precisely is prohibited, nor is there much risk that it will backfire against its supposed beneficiaries.

Although its goals are ambitious, CEDAW is realistic about

implementation: The convention does not aspire to supplant domestic law but instead anticipates that signatories will implement its terms through normal domestic political legislation. Although CEDAW isn't "self-executing," it isn't toothless symbolism either. Compliance with CEDAW is monitored by a multinational group. Every four years, CEDAW's signatories must submit a report to the United Nations Committee on the Elimination of Discrimination against Women, and a national representative must appear before the committee and defend the report. In many ways, CEDAW is an ideal human rights guarantee—it's assertive, yet realistic; it establishes a streamlined international organization to monitor compliance and offer guidance but relies on national governments to handle the details of administration.

In its most recent (2007) report to the committee, Saudi Arabia points out that "[a]ll laws and regulations in force in the Kingdom of Saudi Arabia . . . derive from the Holy Koran and the Sunna of His Messenger, Muhammad. The Holy Koran and immaculate Sunna contain many stipulations prohibiting discrimination on the grounds of race, colour or gender. . . . They contain unequivocal rulings in favor of non-discrimination between men and women, desiring that women enjoy the same rights and duties on a basis of equality."[46] The report contains a long list of laws guaranteeing Saudi women equal rights, a plethora of public policies benefiting women, and a list of women who hold prominent positions in the Saudi government. Moreover, "State authorities are committed, in the performance of their work and exercise of their competence, to the principle of equality between men and women"[47]

This is all welcome news, but one gets a very different impression from the travel advisory of the US Department of State, which warns that women in Saudi Arabia are required by law to veil themselves and wear "a full length black covering known as an Abaya" when in public, are forbidden to drive automobiles, are subject to arrest for prostitution if they are discovered in public with a man who is not a blood relative or husband, and are regularly refused service in restaurants if not accompanied by a man. According to the State Department advisory, these and many other gender-specific prohibitions are enforced by the *Mutawwa*—the religious police who are charged with enforcing conservative standards of public conduct.[48]

The contradiction between the commitment to eliminate all forms of discrimination against women and the persistence of such gender-specific regulation is, according to the Saudi report to CEDAW, only apparent. The report informs us that Saudi law, as guided by the Islamic Sharia, considers all people "equal in respect of a basic humanity which is unaffected by division into sex." But there are practical considerations: "Proceeding from a basis of realism . . . full likeness between men and women is contrary to the reality of . . . the physiological difference between them. . . . Other differences are consequent . . . ," we are informed, "as in respect of inheritance where . . . the male receives double the share of the female. The reason for this is that a man will provide for his wife and children while his sister . . . is not burdened with this outlay but herself will be provided for. . . ." How such differences in responsibilities and privilege are a consequence of physiology is not made clear, but such reasoning is not unique to Saudi Arabia or Sharia law. The Anglo-American common law established sharp distinctions between the marital and inheritance rights of men and women until the mid-twentieth century, and, until the passage of national civil rights legislation in the 1960s and 1970s, many American employers cited the distinctive breadwinning obligations of men as a justification for refusing to hire or promote women in highly remunerative positions. The difference, of course, is that neither the common law nor the employers of the nineteenth and the early twentieth centuries claimed to eschew discrimination against women. Indeed, both celebrated it as necessary and natural.

To the extent any sticklers still find inconsistencies, the Kingdom of Saudi Arabia has made it clear that Sharia law trumps CEDAW, so it ratified the convention "with the reservation that, in cases of contradiction between any term of the Convention and the norms of Islamic law, the Kingdom is not under the obligation to observe the contradictory terms of the Convention." This may seem a prime example of the exception swallowing the rule, but it's unfair to single out Saudi Arabia for special criticism. Numerous other signatories to CEDAW have made similar arguments, ratifying the convention subject to broad general reservations that exempt them from provisions inconsistent with religious law, traditional cultural norms, or other national interests. There's nothing inherently untoward about ratifying a human rights convention subject to reservations—in fact, human rights advocates have long argued that the United States could ratify CEDAW subject to reservations that would ensure consistency with constitutional liberties. Reservations allow for a pragmatic flexibility consistent with the best traditions of international diplomacy. The option of assent subject to reservations can bring reluctant nations into the fold, enlarging the jurisdiction of the convention and improving its legitimacy.

But some reservations can be inconsistent with the central purpose of a convention. Sweeping reservations that exempt signatories from the defining commitments of a convention threaten to turn human rights into hollow gestures. At worst, ratifying a human rights convention may become a matter of good public relations rather than meaningful reform. Legal scholar Oona Hathaway points out that human rights serve an important and often overlooked expressive function: They signal a commitment to humanitarian values that potential trading partners, diplomatic allies, and financial investors may value. But, "when monitoring and enforcement of treaties is minimal . . . the countries that join the treaty will enjoy the expressive benefits of joining . . . regardless of whether they actually comply. . . . Consequently, treaty ratification may become a substitute for, rather than a spur to, real improvement in human rights practices."[49] Many of CEDAW's signatories feel that the integrity of the convention is threatened by an overly permissive approach to carve-outs, such as Saudi Arabia's for Islamic law. Human rights agreements involve an unavoidable tension between inclusiveness and rigor: stringent requirements might yield a convention that only a handful of liberal nations will ratify, but lax or malleable requirements will make it toothless, undermining the very principles for which it stands.

This risk is magnified when the relevant norm is itself ambiguous. Unlike a relatively straightforward human rights guarantee—for instance, a right against torture or political persecution—an antidiscrimination guarantee inevitably involves ambiguities, conflicts, and administrative complexities. Antidiscrimination guarantees that are too broad wind up being swallowed by exceptions, subordinate clauses, and vaguely defined operational terms. CEDAW aspires to eliminate all forms of discrimination against women. *All* forms? Are states to scour the countryside, looking for women's bathrooms and girls' football leagues to dismantle? Must government outlaw Ladies' Night at the local pub (as a few American states have done) and enjoin the anachronistic but harmless male custom of standing when a woman joins a seated group for dinner?

Even the convention's strongest advocates acknowledge that some types of discrimination are reasonable, some even necessary. CEDAW explicitly encourages signatories to take temporary special measures to increase the number of women in traditionally male-dominated spheres, but of course this is straightforward discrimination on the basis of sex. And most people would agree that it's reasonable to mandate that mothers receive longer parental leave from their jobs after the birth of a child than fathers because mothers carry a child to term, give birth, and typically nurse the newborn for several months thereafter.

This is why some women's rights advocates have considered replacing the language of *equality*—which they take to demand formal equal treatment—with the language of *equity*, which would seem to allow for differential treatment when it can be justified. But this kind of terminological shift doesn't really help. General terms such as *equality* and *equity* are both subject to manipulation and multiple interpretations. And to the extent the shift from equality to equity allows for more flexibility, it just trades one problem for another. After all, much inequality can be justified as equitable. For instance, the Saudi government's interpretation of Sharia, which provides sons with double the inheritance of daughters, is arguably equitable when the traditional male familial obligations are taken into consideration. Similarly, an employer's decision to pay men more than women for similar work, while unequal, might be defended as equitable in a society where men are typically breadwinners with families to support and working women typically marry after a few years in the labor market. But of course, those differing roles and obligations themselves reflect the unequal treatment of men and women—hence *equity* can be a way of using past inequality to defend more inequality in the future.

Some advocates have tried to sidestep these difficulties by pointing out that CEDAW prohibits discrimination "against" women; this suggests that CEDAW does not prohibit measures that *help* women but does prohibit those that *harm* women. A sensible rejoinder, but every paternalistic restriction on women's freedom ever devised could be defended as protecting "the fairer sex" from the threat of sexual aggression or the rigors of a hostile man's world. Those who would insist that women—and only women—cover themselves head to toe in a *burqa* often defend their preference by insisting that a glimpse of female flesh threatens to send men into an uncontrolled lascivious frenzy. Shifting from a formal prohibition of discrimination to a policy of women's betterment may be an improvement in terms of substance, but it can be a step back in terms of clarity. And without formal clarity, almost any policy or practice can be made to seem consistent with the human rights mandate. At some point, one must begin to worry that CEDAW has gained widespread universal assent only because its mandate is sufficiently vague and abstract to mean all things to all people. Everyone can agree that they condemn "discrimination against women," but in practice this means very different things depending on national context, local cultural norms, religious commitments, and institutional constraints.

Many countries prohibit discrimination on the basis of race, sex, and other categories with some success, so it may seem to follow that we can extend the same principles to the global theater of human rights. But domestic civil rights laws work best when they borrow from a local tradition of legal rights and a local culture of civic respect and are bolstered by effective domestic legal institutions. For instance, equality of the sexes in American law has developed over the course of decades in a dialogue with other civil rights laws, constitutional principles, and well-established rights to privacy, freedom of expression, and freedom of religion. As a result, American courts, at their best, have interpreted such rights pragmatically, prohibiting the types of discrimination that most undermine women's opportunities while allowing those sex-based distinctions that are too deeply entrenched to be disturbed without destructive social upheaval and counterproductive backlash. For instance, American civil rights laws prohibit discrimination by employers unless sex is a *bona fide occupational qualification*—a term that allows deep-seated notions of sexual privacy occasionally to prevail over strict equality, so that an employer of nurses who must undress and bathe elderly patients can match the sex of the nurse to that of the patient, and an employer can refuse to hire male restroom attendants to provide service in the ladies' room. (Similarly, sensible exceptions to strict equal treatment allow for separate men's and women's restrooms.) Employers are also free to impose different dress codes for male and female employees, provided they impose roughly equal burdens on both sexes, so women can be required to wear skirts and men to wear neckties. Of course, none of these exceptions are necessary and all have been criticized, but they reflect a reasonable effort to balance the prohibition against sex discrimination with widely held and relatively innocuous social norms.

Human rights lawyers hope that international norms defined by human rights will serve a similar function. For instance, legal scholars Abram and Antonia Chayes argued that the need to be accepted into an international community of solidarity and cooperation will provide an incentive to comply with human rights principles.[50] Because such norms are local, there can be no equivalent approach to international human rights. A reasonable approach to women's equality in the Netherlands may well be fantastically ambitious in Sudan. Again, this is a pragmatic

observation. For these purposes, I'm not interested in the question of cultural imperialism or the alleged Western cultural bias
of human rights law. Even if we agree that it would be unequivocally better if women in Sudan were treated more like women in
the Netherlands, and even if we have no ethical qualms about
forcing the Sudanese to conform to the Dutch standard to the
extent we can, the question remains whether human rights can
help us bring the recalcitrant into line with more egalitarian
norms.

As Oona Hathaway worries, acceptance might be earned,
"not only by actual compliance, but also by relatively toothless
expressions of adherence to the relevant norm . . . [w]here . . .
actual changes in practices are . . . difficult to perceive, and
treaty ratification is relatively costless and immediately apparent, ratification may be used to offset pressure for real change."[51]

Perhaps a more promising approach involves working with
national and even municipal governments on the details of
human rights compliance, with attention to the unique challenges and promise of a specific locale. For instance, given the
failure of the United States to ratify CEDAW, some advocates
have bypassed the national government and taken the case to
more receptive local governments. Between 1998 and 2008,
the Women's Institute for Leadership and Development and
Amnesty International worked with the City of San Francisco's Department on the Status of Women to review local
laws and policies for instances of gender bias or inequity. They
collected data on the staffing of city departments and budget
priorities and studied how women used local services. They
discovered that the city could improve job opportunities,
safety, and the provision of services for women by making

some relatively minor and inexpensive changes. For instance, implementing flexible work schedules opened up government jobs to women with child-care responsibilities. When audits of the juvenile justice system revealed that young women who had suffered abuse were a rapidly growing number of juvenile criminal offenders, San Francisco added sexual-abuse counseling to the services offered to troubled youth. And because the study revealed that fear of assault on poorly lit streets restricted the mobility of many women, the city added new streetlights. These small investments paid dividends in terms of gender equity; today, women are well represented in the municipal workforce and run many of San Francisco's most important departments. And the city's gender audit has inspired imitators from as far away as Stockholm and Indonesia. Closer to home, in 2008, fourteen San Francisco businesses pledged to conduct similar gender audits.[52]

The San Francisco experience suggests a new model for substantive or "positive" human rights. Instead of an adversarial relationship to the guarantor of rights, it suggests a cooperative relationship in which state parties look to human rights advocates for new ideas. Instead of a focus on individual entitlements, it suggests a holistic policy approach designed to improve conditions for the greatest number at the least expense. Instead of a set of mandates that may bear little relationship to the institutional capacities of the states obliged to fulfill them, it suggests a flexible and pragmatic method that capitalizes on existing institutional strengths by advocating subtle changes in, and enhancements to, the basic services government already provides. This is, in law professor Janet Halley's terms, a thoroughly "governance"-based approach to human rights. Here the human rights advocate is less an activist pressing an independent agenda and more a consultant, helping to design and implement policy reform.

Much of human rights practice—especially with respect to "positive" welfare rights—seems to be moving in this direction under the rubric of "progressive realization." For instance, the United Nations Right to Food Unit asserts that "programmes and policies regarding the right to food are complex and need good management arrangements; overall the challenges to be addressed are as much institutional as technical."[53] This is an inevitable evolution as human rights advocates take on a larger number of social-welfare questions. The notion of specific entitlements or a rigidly defined set of duties subtly gives way to incremental institutional reform, closer to the method of management science than to that of legal advocacy or political activism. The complexities of an issue such as gender equity demand such a flexible and nuanced approach; the cooperative approach that human rights groups used in San Francisco got results where entitlements, formal demands, or litigation would not have.

But what does such an approach have to do with "rights" as conventionally understood? One wonders whether the expansion of human rights organizations into such new territory requires them to change not only their tactics but also their defining concerns and methods. It's not clear that traditional human rights work—say, political agitation to free prisoners of conscience in authoritarian regimes—has much in common with this kind of consulting. Nor is it clear whether there is any advantage when the same organizations do both kinds of work. And there can be unique risks in thinking of this approach to policy advising in terms of rights. An obvious risk is that, as an adjunct to government, the human rights advocate may become "captured," responding more and more to bureaucratic pressures and political expediencies and less and less to human rights principles: as an agent of government, he will be a poor advocate for human rights. But I suspect the opposite risk may be greater. The advocate will press a narrow human rights agenda to the hilt, with no concern for the vital organs of government he may damage in the thrust. Rather than confront the trade-offs that a responsible policy maker must face, he will imagine that he isn't exercising power at all and hence refuse to accept responsibility for the consequences of his interventions even as he shapes public policy. In other words, as a human rights advocate, he will be an irresponsible policy maker.

For example, as part of its local implementation of CEDAW, San Francisco has made numerous policy changes to benefit women. It may seem to go without saying that these changes further social justice because women have been the victims of discrimination. *But for discrimination, the city would have done all of these things and more long ago*, the argument runs. That *may* be true. But there's no way of knowing with any confidence what the world would look like "but for discrimination." We can be sure that many things would be different, but it's hard to know precisely *which* things would be different, or *how* they would be different. A policy maker can't really try to repair the injuries caused by generations of discrimination; she can only start where she is and try to implement the wisest and most just policies. A policy maker must ask: Were the city's scarce resources best spent on the new streetlights it installed as part of its CEDAW implementation? Were the changes to its employment practices, which increased the number of women working for the city, fair to all concerned?

Talk of human rights doesn't help us to think through these questions—instead, it assumes an answer. Suppose the money the city spent on streetlights ultimately came from the budget to improve playgrounds for children. As a result of the change, four women are spared assaults in the following year (and countless more feel safer and freer to go where they wish at night), but twelve children are injured on rickety playground equipment. Is this a good trade-off? At this point, some readers will resist the hypothetical: The city should install the street-lights *and* fix the playgrounds. Why not raise taxes? Or cut the salaries of overpaid officials? Or eliminate waste? This line of thinking is always congenial: *If we cut the military's budget, we could fund the schools, feed the hungry, and provide universal health care!* But it's usually not realistic. For instance, in the case of San Francisco, the capacity to raise taxes is severely limited by state laws. Almost every politician pledges to cut "waste," but as soon as one tries to do so, influential people who will suffer the cuts make the case that the targeted program is essential, so it avoids the axe. Public unions successfully resist cuts to their constituents' salaries and perks, no matter how lavish, and officials have their salaries and benefits guaranteed in contracts. The easy cuts don't look so easy anymore, and the hard trade-offs have to be made. In such a context (and one very much like it faces every government), human rights might work like a budgetary side-constraint or "earmark": *Cut something else—anything else—but install those streetlights.*

Worse, it might become a way for one constituency or one part of a government bureaucracy to jump the queue in terms of budgetary priorities: If you don't increase funding for sex-abuse counseling or the budget for the Commission on the Status of Women, you are violating human rights. We often think of human rights as a way to control the most recalcitrant governments, but a government that accepts a human rights convention and takes it seriously typically does so because it already has a domestic constituency that supports the agenda in question. The human rights treaty will make it easier for politicians to satisfy this constituency at the expense of others because their preferences will become legal entitlements, while the preferences of other, perhaps less politically powerful, groups will remain optional. Human rights analysis assumes this is a good thing; human rights *should* take first priority. But it is a bad way to make public policy or set budgetary priorities. Rather than taking responsibility for controversial policy decisions, everyone involved can wash his or her hands of the decision. The politicians who have the formal power don't have a choice—human rights require streetlights instead of new playgrounds. The human rights advocates aren't responsible for the trade-offs because they have no formal power. They didn't cut funding for the playgrounds—the politicians did.

To be clear, these cavils are hypothetical. I have no reason to think San Francisco made bad policy decisions or ill-advised budgetary trade-offs at the behest of human rights groups. The San Francisco intervention appears to be an impressive success that one can only hope others will emulate. The language and thinking typical of rights may inspire such laudable efforts, but it is unlikely to guide them in effective or responsible implementation. I suspect that, in many cases, cooperation with local policy makers would be more effective and more responsible if humanitarians abandoned the idea that it has anything to do with rights.

The language of human rights expresses a deep and widespread conviction that some things are too important to be subject to mundane political compromise. It signals an extraordinary consensus among civilized people—regardless of culture, ideology, or structure of government. Communists and capitalists, royalists and republicans, Catholics, Muslims, and secular humanists should all agree that torture, genocide, and slavery are wrong—

wrong unequivocally, always and everywhere. Human rights give us an intellectually rigorous and morally powerful way of expressing the necessary limits of governmental power and the inviolable requirements of human dignity.

In a technologically advanced, economically complex, and geographically interconnected world, however, there is a large and arguably growing number of things that seem indispensable for a decent and fulfilled life. There are also many specific institutional arrangements necessary to secure those things. It's tempting to describe this very large set of political, economic, and administrative relationships in terms of rights, and doing so has some tangible benefits: It focuses public attention on causes that might otherwise go unnoticed and it puts pressure on national governments to improve inhumane conditions within their borders. But there's also a cost to describing a large number of complex and often intractable social problems in terms of rights. The unequivocal moral conviction of rights analysis doesn't make sense in the context of a complex social problem that involves tough judgment calls and trade-offs or a policy intervention that requires administrative sophistication and significant resources.

As a result, the certainty and clarity of rights analysis must subtly give way to the messiness and ambiguity of policy analysis. The strict moral conviction that rights are inalienable must yield to a host of practical cavils and valid excuses for compromise and delay. Inalienable rights become "metrics of institutional capacity for appropriate procedures," and the principle that justice delayed is justice denied yields to "progressive realization." India accepts in principle the right of its citizens to food, but it can't deliver due to logistical bottlenecks, administrative limitations, corruption, and political gridlock. This suggests that rights are negotiable, subject to practical limitations based on expedience. Not that it could be any other way—when one is dealing with the production and distribution of tangible goods, equivocation and "best efforts" necessarily follow. But this makes the next set of equivocations easier to accept. Saudi Arabia can accept in principle the equality of women yet impose countless sex-based exclusions and humiliations in practice. This not only dilutes the meaning of women's equality, it turns the expression of women's rights into a justification for institutionalized male dominance. And, perhaps worst of all, this kind of shift from rights to policy and from policy to politics suggests that rights are an appropriate subject of political manipulation and public relations—just another tool in the belt of the diplomat and the minister of propaganda. This makes it easy for those who find human rights inconvenient to dismiss them as little more than an ideological agenda—as some in the United States did with respect to the torture of prisoners.

CONCLUSION

In order to achieve humanitarian goals most readily and completely, we need to look to the details of local political institutions, cultural norms, civil society, and policy consid erations. Sometimes rights can play an important role in influencing these conditions, but the effectiveness of rights is usually a matter of influence. The real work happens on the ground. In this sense, rights are just tools for making something happen. Sometimes a right is a useful tool—both of analysis and of persuasion—but sometimes it is the wrong tool for the job. It makes sense to put a claim or proposal in terms of rights only when doing so will help us see the issues clearly and/or move the parties to take appropriate action.

Historian Samuel Moyn argues that modern human rights came to prominence only when other political utopian movements—most notably, Marxism and postcolonial self-determination—were discredited. According to Moyn, human rights endured where other utopian visions had failed because they promised an apolitical utopia—one based on uncontroversial moral truths rather than on inevitably contestable political commitments. Some of Moyn's claims are controversial. Many other historians insist that today's human rights are an extension of those established as a response to Nazi atrocities in World War II, or in antislavery activism, or in the great national revolutions of the eighteenth century. But the lesson Moyn draws is instructive regardless: The charisma and prestige of human rights—and their claims to universalism—

depend on their apolitical pretensions. It's plausible that human rights represent universal morality, as opposed to a controversial political agenda, when they are limited to a few of the most serious and discrete abuses. Amnesty International epitomized this limited approach to human rights during its early years with its focus on the imprisonment of political dissidents and its self-conscious aspiration to stay outside—and above—the political and ideological struggles of the day. But as a growing number of issues have come to be defined as questions of human rights, it is harder to think of rights as above or distinct from ordinary politics and ideological conflict. Today's human rights agenda is increasingly a political agenda. At the same time, however, human rights advocates insist that their claims deserve more deference than ordinary political claims. Human rights now straddle morality and politics, seeking the universality and moral priority of the former and the practical scope of the latter.

There are two dangers here. One, on which many commentators have focused, is that the human rights agenda will soil its moral purity as it ventures into the swamp of politics; the political agenda will despoil the moral one. The second, less-discussed danger on which I have focused in this book is that the moral agenda will distort the political one. When political claims are analyzed as if they were moral absolutes, the balancing of interests and questions of expediency that are central to the art of politics yield to unjustified certainty and impractical extremism. To return to an earlier example, it is one thing to insist that it's immoral that millions starve in a world of plenty; it's quite another to press for—even if implicitly and indirectly—a state-run command-and-control distribution of food as the best means of feeding them. The first is an uncontroversial moral truth; the second begs perhaps the single most hotly contested political question of the modern era.

I've argued that the emergence of human rights as the default utopia of the contemporary era raises four pressing questions, and I've looked to an ideologically diverse group of social theorists to help frame those questions. One: Are rights universal? A one-size-fits-all approach to human rights can lead us to ignore the unique needs and limitations of specific societies and to press for changes that are unrealistic or may even do more harm than good. Ultimately, rights must be a part of a local culture of civic virtue and social engagement in order to really make a difference. Two: Can abstract rights guide concrete reforms? Rights express the urgency of certain commitments, but they can also tempt us to ignore the practical impediments and necessary trade-offs of specific institutional change. Three: How do rights affect political consciousness? Rights can shape imagination and self-conception, making more programmatic and comprehensive social change harder to envision and achieve. Four: Can too many rights make a wrong? As human rights language is used to describe a growing number of inherently political concerns, the idea of human rights inevitably is entangled with political disputes and pragmatic compromises. This makes it easier to think of all rights as politically contestable and subject to equivocation—even those that can and should be absolute and inviolable. I haven't aspired to answer these questions definitively—only to pose them in terms that might suggest the need for circumspection.

Following on these questions, I briefly described several controversies in which human rights assertion has played out in specific contexts, each illustrating a challenge for conventional human rights analysis. Many have described the plight of African migrants in Calabria as a human rights issue, and there is no doubt that it is an example of one of the most pressing challenges for humanitarianism today. Moreover, Italy is a prosperous and well-functioning democracy that should be capable of guaranteeing even the most demanding human rights. But if rights require healthy civic customs and norms, rights assertion may be quixotic in a context in which social habits are marked by centuries of distrust and the dominance of organized crime and in which civic institutions are dysfunctional or nonexistent. In Japan, the human rights campaign to stop sex trafficking has led the government to create additional barriers to the migration of women from poor countries, increasing their vulnerability to a class of parasitic migration brokers and facilitators. Is it possible that looking at the issue as one of universal rights distorted the analysis and obscured the costs to these desperate women of a zero-tolerance approach? Could a more pragmatic and less moralistic approach curb truly involuntary migration while facilitating practical improvements for women who see jobs on the fringes of the sex trade as the lesser of evils? The right to food seems, at first glance, among the most important of human rights, but in India, a growing economy and healthy democracy are not enough to overcome corruption, the limits of institutional capacity, and political inertia. Because rights look to the state as the first—and often the only—guarantor, rights assertion has led a bureaucratically overtaxed and politically compromised government to do more, possibly exacerbating the problem by crippling the private market for food. It's possible that the successful distribution of food to the hungry will require the state to do less.

Finally, I looked at a promising development in human rights advocacy, in which advocates work with local institutions and capitalize on local values and customs to develop tailored and holistic ways to achieve humanitarian ends. These approaches still use the rhetoric of individual human rights, but increasingly they shift focus from individual entitlement to the general welfare and from discrete interventions to comprehensive institutional reform. Still, the idea of rights might distort the policy analysis these interventions necessarily entail, allowing a narrow agenda to unjustifiably displace competing concerns. I asked whether these new approaches would be even better if they dropped the idea of rights altogether and proceeded as movements for humanitarian policy reform. Rights now occupy the field of humanitarianism and absorb the imagination of humanitarians, but such a shift might open the door to new ways of thinking and new modes of political and social engagement.

I've come to these questions as an outsider. I'm not active in human rights advocacy other than appearing occasionally at an academic conference, public rally, or event and contributing financially to select organizations. If my comments have merit, it is by virtue of insights derived from my study of jurisprudence, American civil rights, and the perspective of an outsider who lacks an emotional and institutional investment in the well-established human rights approach. In the many discussions I've had with human rights scholars, lawyers, and activists since beginning this book, I've been struck by the consistency of two somewhat contradictory responses. One goes something like this: "But the problems you identify are not problems with the human rights approach—they are the problems of recalcitrant states or poor enforcement. The solution is more aggressive enforcement—not a retreat to a supposedly more flexible, less rigorous policy approach." The other: "We already know about all of these problems, and lots of people and organizations are already working on correcting them. The human rights approach is supple enough to respond to these insights, so you are not really talking about human rights—you are talking about a narrow and outdated approach to human rights."

I don't find either of these responses entirely convincing. As to the first: It's no good to separate human rights from the consistent and predictable reactions to them, just as it would make little sense for a pharmaceutical company to say of an allergic reaction to a new drug: "Those hives and nausea you are suffering are not the fault of our drug; the problem is with your immune system, which mistakes the drug for a dangerous pathogen, triggering an unnecessary immune response." If the reactions are consistent and predictable, they must be treated as characteristic of the approach.

The second reaction is more intriguing. In mundane domestic legal practice, the term *right* has a fairly specific meaning: a legal entitlement that entails a specific duty on the part of a specific entity. The emerging idea of human rights advocacy as a form of governance departs from that definition. The women's rights advocates working in San Francisco didn't press for the recognition of individual claims; instead, they looked for practical improvements that the city could make and they developed useful ways of measuring progress. Similarly, United Nations discussions of the right to food focus on holistic approaches to long-term policy reform and target avaricious financial speculation in food markets as well as laggard states. This suggests the possibility that human rights advocates define "rights" very differently from the way a lawyer working domestically does.

Nevertheless, the language of rights implies individual entitlements and discrete remedies, and it derives its unique persuasive and inspirational power from its association with the authority of formal law. Tellingly, human rights advocacy consistently returns to this conception, even as it struggles to move beyond it. For instance, a report of the United Nations Right to Food Unit focused on the need for holistic institutional approaches tailored to local circumstances, but it still began with the familiar insistence that "states have certain duties that individuals can . . . demand that they carry out. . . ." This isn't surprising because the rhetorical power of rights is hard to separate from this conventional conception. The individualism of rights makes it easier to imagine immediate and discrete remedies; once rights entail collective interests, it's more apparent that cumbersome institutional reform may be required. Likewise, the focus on the state as guarantor provides a discrete target for activism and pressure; without this focus, the source of violations becomes harder to identify, and it's obvious that meaningful change requires unraveling complex relationships—with unpredictable consequences.

Can we separate some of the humanitarian goals now thought of in terms of human rights from the limitations of rights analysis? Why use the language and analysis of human rights when what's really at stake is institutional reform and policy innovation? The "rights approach" has costs, both in terms of defining and potentially distorting analysis and in terms of limiting political imagination of advocates and the people advocacy would serve. These costs should be weighed against the benefits of using the language of rights. In some cases, the balance will favor using rights language, but I suspect that in others where it is currently used, the balance will tilt against a rights approach.

Thinking of rights as tools, rather than as abstract moral imperatives, would encourage us to consider alternative approaches to humanitarianism. And sometimes doing nothing—at least in the short term—might be preferable to taking poorly suited action, even with the best of intentions. For instance, it's now widely believed that humanitarian aid has prolonged many wars and

inadvertently contributed to human suffering and death by providing sustenance and medical aid to combatants. Some observers fear that humanitarian efforts to buy the freedom of slaves
in Sudan drove up the market price and thereby increased the
incentive for slavers to take more captives. It's been reported that
guerrilla forces in Liberia and Sierra Leone deliberately muti-
lated their victims in order to get the attention of the United
Nations and other humanitarian groups: "Without the amputee
factor, you wouldn't have come," insisted one man who spoke
to Dutch journalist Linda Polman. In reaction to such grim
observations, one humanitarian worker complained, "But, good
grief, should we just do nothing at all?"[1] Sadly, in some cases the
answer might be "yes." Similarly, when faced with the personal
story of a woman who has been abducted and forced into sexual
slavery, the natural impulse of anyone with a conscience is to do
something aggressive to prevent such horrors. But it's possible
that what seems to be the most immediate and direct response—
a human rights campaign against sex trafficking—will harm
other innocents. Once one considers *their* interests and needs,
along with those whom human rights assertion might protect, it's
harder to be certain that immediate and direct action is a moral
imperative.

The language of rights is appealing because it suggests that
some things are, or should be, nonnegotiable. Rights offer a
potentially universal moral language—the kind of language that
religion has aspired to provide. It's no accident that the idea
of human rights originated in natural-law theories that were
religious in inspiration. As a result, rights—like religion—can
be a source of conviction and a focus of political organization
for people worldwide, a way of joining millions of potentially
isolated and downtrodden people in common struggle. Human
rights reflect a profound advance in both moral thinking and

political action. But, at the same time, rights suffer from some of the weaknesses of religious thinking: unjustified conviction and blind faith, dogmatism, a priori reasoning (hence, the scholastic theologians believed that one could derive practical moral rules from the metaphysics of the Holy Trinity, and today's rights advocates believe we can derive practical rules of policy administration from the metaphysics of individual moral entitlements), and an impatience with or inattention to practical complexities.

Sadly, our fallen world is not and probably never will be the heaven-on-earth that religious or humanitarian idealists imagine. Much of what can improve it involves the uninspiring details of political negotiation, the mundane techniques of public policy, and day-to day improvements in the efficient production and distribution of goods. To best contribute to these more modest earthly projects, humanitarians must adapt to local politics and scale back ambitious goals in order to avoid undesired side effects and to respect valid competing concerns. And, at times, human rights should cede the field to other movements and modes of thought better suited to the ambiguities of political conflict. To best serve humanity, universal human rights must come down to earth.

ACKNOWLEDGMENTS

My approach in this book has been to marry jurisprudence to journalistic observation—as a result I drew on many diverse sources. My introduction to international human rights questions took place at the groundbreaking NAIL (New Approaches to International Law) conferences held at Harvard Law School during the 1990s. I have found the work of Harvard Law School's David Kennedy especially illuminating—his book *The Dark Sides of Virtue* is an indispensable text. I've also profited a great deal from the work of Harvard's Janet Halley, who writes with rare antidogmatic insight on both domestic and international law—she, more than any other person, has applied rigor, sensitivity, and courage to legal scholarship. My ideas about the limitations of rights analysis owe a great deal to the Critical Legal Studies movement, especially the work of Harvard's Duncan Kennedy and Mark Tushnet; my thoughts about the strengths and necessity of rights owe a great deal to the critical reactions to that work, especially those of Columbia Law School's Patricia Williams and Kimberlé Crenshaw. I found Samuel Moyn's history of human rights, *The Last Utopia*, riveting and full of unexpected observations. I've long admired the work of Kwame Anthony Appiah and found his work on the promise and challenges of cosmopolitanism a background inspiration for this project. I was privileged to meet Rhacel Parreñas, who studied the plight of Filipina hostesses working in Japan, while she was a fellow at Stanford's Center for Advanced Study in the Behavioral Sciences—I was enlightened by her steely analysis of a wrenching social problem and moved by her conviction that the women involved deserve not only sympathy but respect. I learned much about the promise of contemporary human rights practice from conversations with Krishanti Dharmaraj, who has worked with Amnesty International and many other human rights groups. I also profited from several discussions with Karen Engle of the University of Texas School of Law. Finally, I'm most appreciative that Amnesty International approved of this unconventional and unsettling project—a testament to that venerable organization's spirit of intellectual openness.

NOTES

Introduction

1 Edmund Burke, *Reflections on the Revolution in France* (1790), online at http://www.constitution.org/eb/rev_fran.htm.

2 Michel Foucault, "Governmentality," in *The Essential Works of Foucault, 1954–84*, vol. 3, *Power*, ed. James D. Faubion, trans. Robert Hurley (New York: The New Press, 2000), p. 211.

3 See Janet Halley, "Rape at Rome: Feminist Interventions in the Criminalization of Sex-Related Violence in Positive International Criminal Law," *Michigan Journal of International Law* 1 (2008): 3; Janet Halley, Prabha Kotiswaran, Hila Shamir, and Chantal Thomas, "From the International to the Local in Feminist Legal Responses to Rape, Prostitution/Sex Work, and Sex Trafficking: Four Studies in Contemporary Governance Feminism," *Harvard Journal of Law and Gender* 29 (2006): 370–71.

4 Samuel Moyn, *The Last Utopia: Human Rights in History* (Cambridge: Harvard University Press, 2010).

Part One: Rights in Theory

1 Owen Fiss, "Groups and the Equal Protection Clause," *Philosophy and Public Affairs* 5, no. 2 (1976): 107.

2 Gary Orfield, *Reviving the Goal of an Integrated Society: A 21st Century*

Challenge (Los Angeles: The Civil Rights Project/Proyecto Civiles at UCLA, 2009), p. 13.

3 Jeremy Bentham, *Anarchical Fallacies; Being an Examination of the Declarations of Rights Issued During the French Revolution* (1795, 1816), online at http://www.law.georgetown.edu/faculty/lpw/documents/Bentham_Anarchical_Fallacies.pdf.

4 Burke, *Reflections on the Revolution in France.*

5 Ibid.

6 Bentham, *Anarchical Fallacies.*

7 Morton Horwitz, *The Transformation of American Law 1870–1960: The Crisis of Legal Orthodoxy* (New York: Oxford University Press, 1992), p. 155.

8 Olivier De Schutter, "Food for All," Project Syndicate, 1/28/2011, http://www.project-syndicate.org/commentary/deschutter3/English.

9 John Chipman Gray, *The Nature and Sources of the Law*, sec. 48 (1909), according to Wesley Hohfeld, "Some Fundamental Legal Conceptions as Applied in Judicial Reasoning," *Yale Law Journal* 23 (1913): 41.

10 Hohfeld, p. 41.

11 Robert Hale, "Coercion and Distribution in a Supposedly Non-Coercive State," *Political Science Quarterly* 38 (1923): 470.

12 Jeremy Bentham, "A Critical Examination of the Declaration of Rights," in *The Works of Jeremy Bentham*, ed. Sir John Bowring, Vol. 2, part 2 (Edinburgh: William Tait, 1839), p. 501.

13 David Kennedy, *The Dark Sides of Virtue: Reassessing International Humanitarianism* (Princeton, NJ: Princeton University Press, 2004), p. 330.

14 Karl Marx, "On the Jewish Question," in *Karl Marx: Early Writings* (London: Pelican Books, 1975), p. 234.

15 Thomas Paine, *Rights of Man: Being an Answer to Mr. Burke's Attack on the French Revolution*, Part 1 (1791), online at http://www.ushistory.org/paine/rights.

16 Thomas Paine, *The Rights of Man; in two parts* (New York: Vale, 1848), p. 12.

17 Ibid., Part 4.

18 Ibid., Part 16.

19 Ibid.

20 John Yoo, *War by Other Means* (New York: Grove/Atlantic, 2006).

21 See Charles Fried and Gregory Fried, *Because It Is Wrong: Torture, Privacy and Presidential Power in the Age of Terror* (New York: W. W. Norton, 2010).

Part Two: Rights in Practice

1 Nina Burleigh, "African Immigrants in Italy: Slave Labor for the Mafia," *Time,* January 15, 2010 (quoting Roberto Saviano).

2 "Mob Rule: How to Reduce Immigrant Tensions in Italy," *American Foreign Policy*, posted March 28, 2010, http://afpprinceton.com/tag/ndrangheta/.

3 "Rosarno Riots Reopen Immigration Debate," *Italy* magazine, January 11, 2010, http://www.italymag.co.uk/italy/rosarno/rosarno-riots-reopen-immigration-debate.

4 Rachel Donadio, "Race Riots Grip Italian Town and Mafia Is Suspected," *New York Times,* January 10, 2010.

5 John Hopper, "Southern Italian Town World's Only White Town after Ethnic Cleansing," *The Guardian,* January 11, 2010, http://www.guardian.co.uk/world/2010/jan/11/italy-rosarno-violence-immigrants.

6 "Italy: Speed Investigations of Rosarno Attacks: Government Should Signal Zero Tolerance for Racist Violence," Human Rights Watch, February 4, 2010, http://www.hrw.org/en/news/2010/02/04/italy-speed-investigations-rosarno-attacks.

7 Donadio, "Race Riots Grip Italian Town."

8 Jeff Israely, "An Italian Town's White (No Foreigners) Christmas," *Time,* December 1, 2009.

9 Burleigh, "African Immigrants in Italy."

10 Robert D. Putnam, *Making Democracy Work: Civic Traditions in Modern Italy* (Princeton, NJ: Princeton University Press, 1993), p. 144.

11 Roberto Saviano, "Italy's African Heroes," *New York Times,* January 25, 2010.

12 Gaia Pianigiani, "Italy Arrests Hundreds in Mob Sweep," *New York Times,* July 13, 2010.

13 Putnam, p. 124.

14 Ibid., pp. 144–45.

15 Alexis de Tocqueville, *Democracy in America*, Francis Bowen, ed. (Cambridge: Sever and Francis, 1863), pp. 313–14.

16 Putnam, p. 147.

17 See Hohfeld, p. 16.

18 Thomas Paine, *Rights of Man*, Part 1.

19 Robert Burgess and Vikram Haksar, "Migration and Foreign Remittance in the Philippines," IMF Working Paper, June 2005, p. 4.

20 United Nations Protocol to Prevent, Suppress and Punish Trafficking in Persons (TIP), Especially Women and Children, Article 3(a).
21 See Elizabeth Bernstein, "The Sexual Politics of the 'New Abolitionism'," *Differences* 18, no. 3 (2007): 128.
22 Philip Shenon, "Feminist Coalition Protests U.S. Stance on Sex Trafficking Treaty," *New York Times,* January 13, 2000.
23 See Ibid.; Brian Blomquist, " 'Hooker' Panel Puts First Lady on the Spot," *New York Post,* January 8, 2000; William J. Bennett and Charles W. Colson, "The Clintons Shrug at Sex Trafficking," *Wall Street Journal,* January 10, 2000.
24 Trafficking in Persons Report 2004, p. 14.
25 Ibid., pp. 96–97.
26 Rhacel Salazar Parreñas, "Trafficked? Filipino Hostesses in Tokyo's Nightlife Industry," *Yale Journal of Law and Feminism* 18, no. 1 (2006): 163.
27 Elisabeth Bumiller, "Evangelicals Sway White House on Human Rights Issues Abroad," *New York Times,* October 26, 2003, p. A1.
28 Trafficking Victims Protection Reauthorization Act of 2003, H.R. 2620, 108th Cong. (2003), section 7.
29 Halley et al., "From the International to the Local in Feminine Legal Responses."
30 Ibid., pp. 347–60.
31 Amy Waldron, "Poor in India Starve as Surplus Wheat Rots," *New York Times,* December 2, 2002.
32 Ibid.
33 Erika Kinetz, "Wheat Rots in India as Global Prices Hit 2 Year High, Plenty but Not for the Hungry," *Los Angeles Times,* August 6, 2010.
34 Eric de Carbonnel, "The Truth About India's Wheat Reserves," March 23, 2010, http://www.marketskeptics.com/2010/03/truth-about-indias-wheat-reserves.html.
35 Sachin Kumar Jain, "Unfolding Public Distribution System in Madhya Pradesh" (2005), www.righttofoodindia.org/data/jainpdsarticle.doc.
36 Planning Commission, Government of India, "Performance Evaluation of Target Public Distribution System," March 2005, http://planningcommission.nic.in/reports/peoreport/peo/peo_tpds.pdf, p. v. See also George Cheriyan, "Enforcing the Right to Food in India: Bottlenecks in Delivering the Expected Outcome," United Nations University

World Institute for Development Economics Research, November 2006, p. 13.

37 Jain, op. cit.

38 Jim Yardley, "India Asks, Should Food Be a Right for the Poor?" *New York Times,* August 8, 2010.

39 Cheriyan, "Enforcing the Right to Food in India," p. 7.

40 Food and Agriculture Organization of the United Nations, "The Right to Food in Practice: Implementation at the National Level," Rome, 2006, p. 2.

41 Sameer Dossani, "Amnesty International Responds to 'Poverty Is Not a Human Rights Violation," *Aid Watch* (blog), June 5, 2009, http:// aidwatchers.com/2009/06/amnesty-international-responds-to-pov erty-is-not-a-human-rights-violation/.

42 Yardley, "India Asks, Should Food Be a Right for the Poor?"

43 Arvind Virmani, "Poverty and Hunger in India: What Is Needed to Eliminate Them. Working Paper No. 1/2006-PC," Planning Commission, Government of India, February 2006, p. 16; Arvind Virmani and P. V. Rajeev, "Excess Food Stocks, PDS and Procurement Policy. Working Paper No. 5/2002-PC," Planning Commission, Government of India, May 2002, pp. 6–8.

44 Ibid.

45 William Easterly, "Poverty Is not a Human Rights Violation," June 5, 2009, http://aidwatchers.com/2009/06/poverty-is-not-a-human-rights-violation/.

46 Committee on the Elimination of Discrimination against Women, "Consideration of reports submitted by States Parties under article 18 of the Convention on the Elimination of All Forms of Discrimination against Women," Saudi Arabia, March 27, 2007, p. 7 (hereafter, CEDAW Report: Saudi Arabia).

47 CEDAW Report: Saudi Arabia, p. 13.

48 International Travel, Saudi Arabia Country Specific Information, US Department of State, Bureau of Consular Affairs, http://travel .state.gov/travel/cis_pa_tw/cis/cis_1012.html.

49 Oona A. Hathaway, "Do Human Rights Treaties Make a Difference?" *Yale Law Journal* 111, no. 8 (June 2002): 1935, 2006, 2009.

50 See, generally, Abram Chayes and Antonia Handler Chayes, *The New Sovereignty: Compliance with International Regulatory Agreements* (Cambridge: Harvard University Press, 1995).

51 Hathaway, p. 2016.

52 See http://www.imow.org/wpp/stories/viewStory?storyId=1849.

53 Food and Agriculture Organization of the United Nations, "The Right to Food in Practice," p. 20.

Conclusion

1 Philip Gourevitch, "Alms Dealers: Can You Provide Humanitarian Aid without Facilitating Conflicts?" *The New Yorker,* October 11, 2010.

INDEX